THE PRINCIPLES OF LEGAL LIABILITY FOR TRESPASSES AND INJURIES BY ANIMALS

THE PRINCIPLES OF LEGAL LIABILITY FOR TRESPASSES AND INJURIES BY ANIMALS

BY

WILLIAM NEWBY ROBSON,

M.A., LL.B. (Cantab.), LL.B. (Victoria), LL.D. (Leeds)

Solicitor of the Supreme Court

Sometime Scholar of Gonville and Caius College, Cambridge

Cambridge:

at the University Press

1915

CAMBRIDGE
UNIVERSITY PRESS

University Printing House, Cambridge CB2 8BS, United Kingdom

Cambridge University Press is part of the University of Cambridge.

It furthers the University's mission by disseminating knowledge in the pursuit of education, learning and research at the highest international levels of excellence.

www.cambridge.org
Information on this title: www.cambridge.org/9781107456518

© Cambridge University Press 1915

First published 1915
First paperback edition 2014

A catalogue record for this publication is available from the British Library

ISBN 978-1-107-45651-8 Paperback

PREFACE

THE law governing cases of wrongs committed by means of animals is difficult and obscure. This is due to the fact that cases upon the subject are not numerous and, as a rule, the topic is only dealt with incidentally in books on the Law of Torts. The consequent lack, both of authority and opinion, leads both to inconsistency and uncertainty.

This book aims at a systematic exposition of the principles underlying the law, by examining their origin and development and explaining their present application. It is hoped that it will prove of service to practitioners and also to those who are interested in theories of law.

The author desires to express his thanks to Professor Courtney Kenny who suggested to him the need for such a work and also to his friend Mr Roland Burrows, M.A., LL.D., of the Inner Temple, Barrister-at-Law, for much valuable advice during the preparation of this book.

SUNDERLAND.
January, 1915.

TABLE OF CONTENTS

TABLE OF CASES

TABLE OF REFERENCES

Abbreviations	Reports	Dates
A.C.	Law Reports, House of Lords and Privy Council Appeal Cases.	1891–
Ad. & El. ⎱ A. & E. ⎰	Adolphus & Ellis.	1834–1841.
B. & Ald.	Barnewall & Alderson.	1817–1822.
B. & C.	Barnewall & Creswell.	1822–1830.
B. & S.	Best & Smith.	1861–1869.
Beav.	Beavan.	1836–1866.
Bing.	Bingham.	1822–1840.
Burr.	Burrow.	1756–1772.
C.B.	Common Bench.	1845–1856.
C.B. (N.S.).	Common Bench, New Series.	1856–1865.
C. & P.	Carrington & Payne.	1823–1841.
Camp.	Campbell.	1807–1818.
Car. & K. ⎱ Car. & Kir. ⎰	Carrington & Kirwan.	1843–1850.
Co. Rep.	Coke.	1572–1616.
C.M. & R.	Crompton, Meeson & Roscoe.	1834–1836.
Cro. Eliz.	Croke, of the reign of Elizabeth.	
Cro. Jac.	,, ,, ,, James.	
Cro. Car.	,, ,, ,, Charles.	
Dowl.	Dowling.	1830–1842.
East.	East.	1801–1812.
Esp.	Espinasse.	1793–1806.
Exch.	Exchequer.	1847–1856.
Ex. D. ⎱ Exch. Div. ⎰	Law Reports, Exchequer Division.	1875–1891.
F. & F.	Foster & Finlason.	1856–1867.

Abbreviations	Reports	Dates
H. & N.	Hurlstone & Norman.	1856–1862.
H.L. Cas.	House of Lords Cases.	1846–1866.
Holt. (N.P.).	Holt's Nisi Prius.	1815–1817.
H. Bl. ⎫ Hy. Bl. ⎬	Henry Blackstone.	1788–1796.
Ir. R.	Law Reports, Ireland.	(Current)
I.L.T.	Irish Law Times.	„
J.P.	Justice of the Peace.	„
Jon. W.	See W. Jo.	
Jur.	Jurist.	1837–1854.
[190–] K.B.	Law Reports, King's Bench Division	1901– .
Keb.	Keble.	1661–1679.
L.J. (C.P.)	Law Journal, Common Pleas.	⎫
L.J. (Ex.)	„ „ Exchequer.	⎪
L.J. (K.B.) or (Q.B.).	„ „ King's or Queen's Bench.	⎬ 1828– .
L.J. (O.S.).	„ „ Old Series.	⎭
L.R.C.P.	Law Reports, Common Pleas Cases.	⎫
L.R. Exch.	„ „ Exchequer Cases.	⎪
L.R.H.L.	„ „ English & Irish Appeals.	⎬ 1865–1875.
L.R.Q.B.	„ „ Queen's Bench Cases.	⎭
L.T.	Law Times Reports.	(Current)
Lat. ⎫ Latch. ⎬	Latch.	1625–1628.
Ld Raym.	Lord Raymond.	1694–1732.
Lev.	Levinz.	1660–1696.
Lut. ⎫ Lutw. ⎬	Lutwyche.	1682–1704.
M. & W.	Meeson & Welsby.	1836–1847.
Mod. ⎫ Mod. Rep. ⎬	Modern Reports.	1660–1732.
Moo.	Moore.	1512–1631.
Moo. P.C.C.	Moore's Privy Council Cases.	1836–1862.
Moo. P.C.C. (N.S.).	Moore's Privy Council Cases. New Series.	1862–1873.
Moo. & P.	Moore & Payne.	1828–1831.

Abbreviations	Reports	Dates
Poph.	Popham.	1592–1627.
Q.B.	Queen's Bench.	1841–1852.
[189–] Q.B.	Law Reports, Queen's Bench Division.	1891– .
Q.B.D.	Law Reports, Queen's Bench Division.	1875–1890.
Salk.	Salkeld.	1689–1712.
Scott.	Scott.	1834–1840.
Scott (N.R.).	Scott's New Reports.	1840–1845.
Stark.	Starkie.	1815–1822.
St. Tr.	State Trials.	1163–1820.
Str. ⎫ Stra. ⎬	Strange.	1716–1749.
T.L.R.	Times Law Reports.	1884– .
Taunt.	Taunton.	1807–1819.
Ventr.	Ventris.	1660–1691.
W. Jo.	Sir William Jones.	1620–1640.
W.R.	Weekly Reporter.	1882–1906.
Wils.	Wilson.	1742–1774.
Wm. Bl.	William Blackstone.	1746–1779.
Y. & J.	Younge & Jervis.	1826–1830.

INTRODUCTION

Before entering upon an examination of the principles of legal liability for trespasses and injuries by animals it is necessary to classify animals themselves, for liability depends in all cases upon the kind of animal which is the cause of the wrong complained of.

English law, following the Civil law, distinguishes between "animals ferae naturae" and "animals mansuetae or domitae naturae," the former class including all "wild animals" (in the popular sense) whether of a dangerous nature or otherwise, the latter class comprising all tame or domestic animals. The classification is primarily for the purpose of determining rights of property in animals, domestic animals alone being the subject of absolute ownership. But the classification is also at the root of liability for trespass by animals to land.

Our law recognises a further classification in determining the principles of liability for injuries by animals. According to this classification, animals may be either first, those which are of a naturally ferocious, dangerous or mischievous disposition; or secondly, those which are not of such a disposition. The latter the law assumes not to be dangerous, either because they are universally recognised as being of a harmless disposition or because they have acquired a harmless disposition in this country by being domesticated for generations. Evidence will be received to show that a class of animals, hitherto accounted dangerous, has become domesticated and tamed in the course of time.

Considering first the question of trespass to land, it may be stated in general terms that no action will lie for the trespass to land of "animals ferae naturae." But, in connection with this, where such animals are brought or collected upon land in numbers greater than such land can reasonably and properly support, presumably an action will lie for the damage resulting from their escape. "Overstocking," as this has been called, is a nuisance, and to establish liability it must be proved that (1) the increase of animals is "artificial," not natural; (2) the defendant has gone beyond what is reasonable to enable him to have the natural and lawful use and enjoyment of his land; and (3) damage has occurred over and beyond that which ordinarily results from the trespass of such animals.

The person who tames or reclaims an animal which is usually found in a wild state in this country is liable for any trespass committed by it, and for the natural and ordinary consequences of such trespass. But this responsibility ceases when the animal has escaped and reverted to its wild state. Whether in any particular case it has so reverted is a question of fact.

The owner of domestic animals is under a duty to prevent them from trespassing on the lands of others. This duty is absolute, and therefore it is immaterial whether he has exercised proper care and caution in the matter. But his liability, on the other hand, extends only to the "natural and probable" conse-

quences of the trespass and not to consequences
legally too remote.

The liability for trespass of animals is excluded
where the trespass complained of is involuntary, or is
due to vis major or the act of God; or is occasioned by
the omission of a third person whose duty it was to
keep a fence in repair and over whom the defendant
had no control; or is the fault of the plaintiff who,
being under a legal duty to fence out the defendant's
cattle, omits to fence; or is committed from a highway
where the animals are lawfully passing.

In considering the case of injuries to the person and
other animals and of damage to goods, the principles
of liability group themselves under three heads: the
absolute duty of preventing harm, the duty of exercising care to prevent harm, and certain other duties
conveniently considered in this connection, the chief
of which are the positive duty of giving warning of
the probable occurrence of harm, and the negative
duty of refraining from the creation of anything in
the nature of a concealed source of harm.

Dealing first with the absolute duty: a person who
keeps an animal of a species well recognised to be
ferocious, dangerous or mischievous, keeps it at his
peril, and is liable for the consequences of any act of
harm committed by it. Proof of negligence is unnecessary, as negligence is presumed by the law. The
person who keeps such an animal is also taken to be
cognisant of its dangerous nature, and proof that he
had good reason to believe that the particular animal
was docile and harmless will not affect his liability
but may be tendered in reduction of damages.

Whether the mere keeping a dangerous animal is a wrongful act is a question to which the early authorities give a clear answer in the affirmative. More recently, doubts have been entertained by the courts as to the soundness of such authorities.

The person who keeps a domestic or harmless animal is not liable (apart from negligence or trespass) for harm caused by acts which the animal has a natural tendency to commit; nor is he liable at common law for acts of a vicious or mischievous nature, unless proof be given that he knew, at the time of the act complained of, that the animal possessed a propensity or disposition to commit acts of that character. Proof of such knowledge is technically called "proof of the scienter." Apart from Statute, liability does not depend upon ownership but upon possession. The person who "keeps" the animals is the responsible party.

In proving the scienter, knowledge must be shown of a propensity or disposition of the particular animal to commit acts of the kind which has effected the injury or caused the damage complained of. Evidence of scienter, generally speaking, must tend to establish knowledge of that particular propensity, not of some disposition equally obnoxious.

By the Dogs Act 1906 (repealing and re-enacting with some modifications the Dogs Act 1865) the owner of a dog is rendered liable for injuries done by it to cattle, including horses, mules, asses, sheep, goats and swine; and the complainant is exempted from proving scienter or negligence on the part of such owner. Further, where any such injury has been done, the occupier of premises where the dog was kept or permitted to live or remain at the time of the injury is presumed to be the owner of the dog and is liable for the injury unless he proves that he was not the owner of the dog at that time. In case there are several occupiers, as where the premises are let in separate apartments or lodgings or otherwise, the occupier of that part of the premises in which the dog has been kept or permitted to live or remain at the time of the injury is presumed to be the owner of the dog. If the damages claimed do not exceed £5, proceedings for recovery of the same may be taken under the Summary Jurisdiction Acts as for a civil debt.

Scienter may be established by proof of knowledge on the part of a servant or agent, if the person who keeps the animal has delegated to his servant or agent either the management of his business (so as to make it the duty of the servant to communicate his knowledge to his master), or the control of the animal which caused the injury.

Assuming that the other conditions of liability are present, it is immaterial whether the harm complained of is an injury to the person or damage to property (including other animals), or whether it occurs on the premises where the animal is kept, or on the premises of the plaintiff or any other person, or on the highway.

The absolute liability is excluded where the injury is caused by vis major or the act of God (sed quaere); where the immediate cause of the injury complained of was the act of a third person; where the plaintiff suffers by his own default or brings the injury upon himself, or where he, knowing of the risk of harm, voluntarily undertakes it; or where the plaintiff, at the time of the injury complained of, was trespassing upon the premises where the animal was kept.

The person who has kept a dangerous animal presumably remains responsible after it has escaped for all acts of harm committed by it, if it is one of a class not usually found at large in this country. If it is of a class which usually is found at liberty, then, it is submitted, the responsibility for its future acts ceases as soon as the animal has returned to its natural state sine animo revertendi.

With reference to negligence, a person who keeps an animal is liable for harm caused by it, or through its instrumentality, in any circumstances in which the law raises a duty of taking care in the control of the animal on the part of that person, and there has been a breach of that duty. Liability extends to the natural and probable consequences of the breach of duty, but not to an unexpected event.

The circumstances in which such a duty arises cannot be classified, but the commonest case is where an animal is on the highroad accompanied by a person under whose control it purports to be. Here care must be exercised to prevent harm to others occurring through the animal entering on private property or coming in contact with passengers on the highway.

There is no duty at common law on the part of an occupier of land adjoining a highway to fence his land so as to prevent his animals from straying on the highway. Such an occupier is therefore not liable for negligence if an animal of his, not known to him to be dangerous, strays on the highway and there causes damage. But where animals are allowed to stray on a highway in such numbers or under such circumstances as to cause an obstruction and to make the highway unsafe and dangerous to the persons using it, an action will lie.

Where premises are rendered unsafe by reason of the fact that the occupier keeps an animal there which is of a dangerous disposition, the occupier is under a duty to take reasonable care to prevent harm which he knows or ought to know is likely to occur to persons who enter upon the premises at his invitation, express or implied. But where persons enter upon such premises by the mere permission of the occupier, the duty of the latter is no more than to give warning of the dangerous character of the animal.

A person who lets out for hire an animal which he knows or ought to know is dangerous is under a duty to warn, not only the person who hires it, but also any person who he knows or contemplates or ought to contemplate will use it, and such duty is independent of contract.

PART I

THE CLASSIFICATION OF ANIMALS

1. (1) English law distinguishes between animals ferae naturae and animals mansuetae or domitae naturae. The former class includes all wild animals, whether of a dangerous nature or otherwise. The latter class comprises all tame or domestic animals.

(2) The purpose of the classification is primarily for the determination of rights of property in animals.

(3) The same classification is the ground of liability for the trespass of animals.

(1) The English law has adopted the same classification of animals as that which obtained in the Civil law. Animals ferae naturae include all wild animals, whether they are of a ferocious or mischievous nature or not. Thus lions, tigers, bears (Besozzi v. Harris [1858], 1 F. & F. 92), wolves, elephants (Filburn v. The People's Palace and Aquarium Company Ltd [1890], 25 Q.B.D. 261), monkeys (May v. Burdett [1846], 9 Q.B. 101), rabbits, deer (Brady v. Warren [1900] 2 I.R. 632) and pigeons, are to be reckoned as

animals ferae naturae. Animals mansuetae or domitae naturae comprise all tame and domestic animals such as cats (Clinton v. J. Lyons & Co. [1912], 3 K.B. 198), dogs (Read v. Edwards [1864], 17 C.B. (N.S.) 245), horses (Cox v. Burbidge [1863], 13 C.B. (N.S.) 430), cattle and others of a like nature.

The distinction between the two classes has no reference to the proclivities of the animal itself; for on the one hand many animals ferae naturae (e.g. rabbits) are universally recognised to be of a harmless disposition, and on the other hand many animals undoubtedly domitae naturae are addicted to acts of a nature harmful to property.

The law is also said to distinguish between animals ferae naturae "fit for the food of man" and those which are not. (Hannam v. Mockett [1824], 2 B. & C. 934.) But here the true distinction seems to be between those animals which under normal circumstances enjoy a state of natural liberty and those which are usually found living in association with man.

Some writers assume that all animals were originally wild and continued so until brought into a state of subjection by man. Thus Blackstone remarks: "Under this head (animals ferae naturae) some writers have ranked all the former species of animals we have mentioned (animals mansuetae or domitae naturae) apprehending none to be originally and naturally tame, but only made so by art and custom, as horses, swine, and other cattle; which if originally left to themselves would have chosen to rove up and down, seeking their food at large, and are only made domestic by use and familiarity; and are therefore, say they, called mansuetae quasi manui assueta. But however well this notion may be founded, abstractedly considered, our law apprehends the most obvious distinction to be, between such animals as we generally see tame, and are therefore seldom, if ever, found wandering at large, which it calls domitae naturae: and such creatures as are usually found at liberty, which are therefore supposed to be more emphatically ferae naturae, though it may happen that the latter shall be sometimes tamed and confined by the art and industry of man. Such as are deer in a park, hares or rabbits in an enclosed warren, doves in a dove-house, pheasants or partridges in a mew, hawks that are fed and commanded by their owner, and fish in a private pond or in tanks." (Comm. Bk 11, c. 35.)

Tamed animals are separately classed by Bracton as "animalia mansueta," and for some purposes this treatment might well be retained. It seems that domestic animals which gain their freedom and eventually become wild are classed as animals ferae naturae. (Falkland Islands Co. v. Reg. [1863] 2 Moo. P.C.C. (N.S.) 266.)

(2) Domestic animals are the subject of absolute property. They are in the same category as chattels. The right of ownership is retained in them even though they are lost, and an action of trover will lie for their recovery. (Binstead v. Buck [1777], 2 Wm Bl. 1117.) An action of trespass may also be maintained for taking them or carrying them away. "An action of trover doth lie where a trespass doth not and if the plaintiff hath mistaken his action, that shall be no bar to him. ....If a man bring trespass for the taking of a horse

and is barred in that action, yet if he can get the
horse in his possession, the defendant in the trespass
can have no remedy, because, notwithstanding such
recovery, the property is still in the plaintiff." But a
recovery in trespass is a good plea in bar to an action
of trover for the same taking. (Putt v. Roster [1682],
2 Mod. Rep. 319.)

Animals ferae naturae, while living, are not the
subject of absolute ownership. They are not reckoned
as a man's goods and chattels but pass with his free-
hold. They may be his "ratione soli" or "ratione
privilegii" by reason of a park or warren. Moreover,
a "qualified" property is said to be acquired in animals
ferae naturae by taking or taming them (Sutton v.
Moody [1697], 1 Ld. Raym. 250), and a "possessory
property" subsists in the young of animals ferae
naturae whilst they are on a person's land and have
not yet acquired the capacity of flight.

Case of Swans ([1591] 7 Co. Rep. 15). "In this case
it was resolved, that in some of them which are ferae
naturae, a man hath jus proprietatis, a right of property; and in some of them a man hath jus privilegii,
a right of privilege. And there are three manner of
rights of property: scil. property absolute, property
qualified, and property possessory. A man hath not
absolute property in anything which is ferae naturae,
but in those which are domitae naturae. Property
qualified and possessory a man may have in those
which are ferae naturae; and to such property a man
may attain by two ways: by industry, or ratione
impotentiae et loci; by industry as by taking them, or
by making them mansueta, i.e. manui assueta, or

domesticae, i.e. domui assueta; but in those which
are ferae naturae, and by industry are made tame, a
man hath but a qualified property in them, scil. so
long as they remain tame, for if they do attain to their
natural liberty, and have not animum revertendi, the
property is lost; ratione impotentiae et loci, as if a
man has young shovelers or goshawks, or the like,
which are ferae naturae, and they build in my land, I
have possessory property in them, for if one takes them
when they cannot fly, the owner of the soil shall have
an action of trespass....But when a man hath savage
beasts ratione privilegii, as by reason of a park, warren,
etc., he hath not any property in the deer, or conies, or
pheasants, or partridges; and therefore in an action,
quare parcum warrennum etc. fregit et intrav', et 3
damas, lepores, cuniculos, phasianos, perdices, cepit
et asportavit, he shall not say suos for he hath no
property in them, but they do belong to him ratione
privil' for his game and pleasure, so long as they remain
in the privileged place."

With regard to jura proprietatis in animals ferae
naturae such as are termed game, the word "property"
can mean no more than the exclusive right to catch,
kill, and appropriate such animals, which is sometimes
called by the law a reduction of them into possession.
(Blades v. Higgs [1865], 11 H.L.Cas. 621.)

At common law there could be no larceny of dogs,
by reason of the "baseness of their nature"; nor of
such tamed or reclaimed animals as "serve not for
food but pleasure," such as bears, foxes, or ferrets;
but an action of trespass can be maintained in respect
of them. (1 Hale P.C. 512.) It seems also that an action

of trover will lie for any reclaimed animal. (Com. Dig. Action sur Trover, C.)

(3) The trespass of animals was, under the old practice, remediable in an action of trespass and not by means of an action on the case. The writ of trespass, moreover, was available only in the case of those animals in which a right of property could exist at common law. Hence the practical result was that to ascertain whether a remedy could be had it was necessary first to classify the animal.

2. (1) English law recognises a further classification in determining the principles of liability for injuries by animals. Here, animals may be classed in two divisions according to their propensities or disposition, namely: first, those animals which are of a naturally ferocious, dangerous or mischievous, though possibly reclaimable disposition; and secondly, those animals which are of a harmless disposition.

(2) The classification does not depend on rights of property in animals. This being so, it is better to adopt the terms "dangerous animals" and "harmless animals," or kindred general expressions, to denote the respective classes in preference to the terms "animals ferae naturae" and "animals domitae or mansuetae naturae" which are commonly employed for that purpose.

(3) "Harmless animals," in the sense used
in the previous paragraph, includes all animals
which are universally recognised as being not
originally by nature dangerous, and all animals which in this country have acquired a
harmless disposition by being domesticated
for generations.

(4) The courts will take judicial notice of
the fact that certain animals belong to the
class of dangerous animals or to the class of
harmless animals.   Evidence will be received
to show that a species of animals hitherto
accounted as of the dangerous class, has, by
the habits or training of generations, become
tame and domesticated, and therefore ranks
with the harmless class of animals.

In treating of injuries by animals the principles of
liability are found to rest upon a distinction between
those animals which are and those which are not of a
dangerous nature.   The name "animals ferae naturae"
is habitually applied to the former class, though it and
the corresponding English term "wild animals" are
ambiguous and misleading.

The basis of the classification and the rules of law
thereon founded are well put by Lord Esher M.R. in
his judgment delivered in Filburn v. The People's
Palace and Aquarium Co. Ltd ([1890], 59 L.J. (Q.B.)
471), a case of injury by an elephant. "There is no
doubt that the law of England recognises two distinct

classes of animals. With regard to one class, a person
who keeps an animal of that class must keep it at his
peril, and prevent it from doing injury; and whether
he knows it to be dangerous or not is immaterial.
There is another class of animals which the law assumes
not to be of a dangerous nature, although individuals
of that class may become dangerous, and a person who
keeps an animal of that class is not liable for injury done
by it unless he knew that the individual animal was
dangerous. What is the best formula for determining
to which particular class a particular animal belongs?
There are some animals which it is well known are not
originally by nature dangerous, and which the law
recognises as not being dangerous, and it is immaterial
whether they have become domesticated or not.
Whether they are ferae naturae, as not being the
subject of property, is not the point. Thus, rabbits,
hares, pheasants, partridges, and the like, are ferae
naturae in the sense that they do not belong to anyone
until they have been reduced into possession, but
they are not ferae naturae in the sense that they are
dangerous. There is another set of animals which
the law has recognised as not being of a dangerous
nature in England; these are cows, oxen, horses, dogs,
sheep, and many others, which I need not attempt to
enumerate. How has that recognition come about?
Some of these animals originally, whether in this
country or elsewhere, in their wild state were dangerous,
but a great many years ago the whole race of animals
of that kind in this country was so tamed that it is
known as a matter of fact that their progeny are not
dangerous, and they are recognised not to be dangerous.

The animals I have mentioned are recognised by the law of England as not being of a dangerous nature because of such universal knowledge, and the law assumes without further proof that such animals are not of a dangerous nature.... Unless, therefore, an animal can be brought within one or other of those recognised classes—namely, animals which are nowhere dangerous, or animals which have come to be recognised in England as not being of a dangerous nature—it must be treated as an animal belonging to the class of animals which must be kept from doing mischief, and such animal would come within the first and not the second class." The Court held that, as an elephant could not be said to be not dangerous by nature nor domesticated in this country, it must be reckoned as a dangerous animal.

Whether a particular animal belongs to one or the other class seems to be a question of law. The Court will take judicial notice of the fact that certain animals belong to the class of dangerous animals in this country; such as lions and tigers (Rex v. Huggins [1730], 2 Ld Raym. 1583), bears (Besozzi v. Harris [1858], 1 F. & F. 92), wolves, elephants and monkeys (May v. Burdett [1846], 9 Q.B. 101). Bees apparently are not animals ferae naturae in this sense. (O'Gorman v. O'Gorman [1903] 2 Ir. Rep. 573.)

From the few cases which have occurred of injuries following the keeping of dangerous animals it seems that the courts will refrain from enumerating such animals generally, but will be content to decide the question in each new case as it arises; and from the remarks of Lindley L.J. in Filburn's case it appears that evidence would be accepted to show that a species of animals, hitherto accounted as of the dangerous class, has become so tamed and domesticated that it is known as a matter of fact that their progeny are not dangerous, and that they are recognised not to be dangerous. In this event the species would fall within the rules governing the class of harmless animals.

PART II

TRESPASS TO LAND

Section I. *By animals ferae naturae*

1. No action will lie for the trespass of animals ferae naturae.

For damage caused by rabbits or hares or other like animals which escape from my land into yours, I am not responsible; for you may capture or kill them at your pleasure.

Mich. 39 and 40 Eliz. In the Common Pleas. "Between Boulston and Hardy it was adjudged in the Common Pleas, that if a man makes coney-boroughs in his own land, which increase in so great number that they destroy his neighbour's land next adjoining, his neighbour cannot have an action on the case against him who makes the said coney-boroughs; for so soon as the coneys come on his neighbour's land he may kill them, for they are ferae naturae, and he who makes the coney-boroughs has no property in them, and he shall not be punished for the damage which the coneys do in which he has no property, and which the other may lawfully kill" ([1597], 5 Co. Rep. 104 *b*). A more detailed report of this case may be found in Cro. Eliz. 547.

To the same effect is Hinsley v. Wilkinson (Cro. Car. 387), where it was held that a commoner could not maintain an action for damage done by the rabbits of another upon the common.

Boulston's case is cited with approval by Bayley J. in delivering the judgment of the full Court of King's Bench in Hannam v. Mockett ([1824], 2 B. & C. 939), and must now be regarded as settled law on this point. See Brady v. Warren ([1900] 2 Ir. Rep. 632).

It is noticeable that in the principal case the injury was brought about by defendant's own active interference. He it was who made the "boroughs" and stocked the conies. The principle of the case is clear enough, but the facts are wide enough to cover the exception contained in the next following rule and it is a difficult matter to reconcile the two.

2.   But where such animals are brought on land in numbers greater than such land can reasonably and properly support, it seems that an action will lie for the damage resulting from their escape. The ground of action (if such an action does lie) is nuisance, and to establish liability it is essential that:

(*a*) the increase in numbers of the animals be caused by the act of the defendant. For damage resulting from a natural increase no action will lie.

(*b*) defendant shall have gave beyond what is reasonable to enable him to have the

2—2

natural and lawful use and enjoyment of his land.

(c) proof be given of damage over and beyond that which ordinarily results from the trespass of such animals.

If there be wild animals in my close, whether there naturally or brought there by me, I am not responsible for their trespass to the land of another. But if I cause game to be brought on my land or if I artificially accumulate them so that their numbers become greater than my close may reasonably support, and by reason of this "non-natural" increase, so to speak, the animals are crowded out and escape into your lands and cause damage there, this, it seems, is a nuisance for which I am answerable.

In Farrer v. Nelson ([1885], 15 Q.B.D. 258) where land was let to a tenant reserving the right of shooting over it, it was held that the tenant was able to maintain an action against the persons entitled to the shooting rights for overstocking the land with game so as to cause damage to the tenant's crops. In that case Baron Pollock said: "I will first deal with the question whether an action can be brought by a neighbour against any person who collects animals upon his land so as to injure the crops of the neighbour, and I should say that beyond doubt such an action would lie, and that the rule upon which it would be founded would be not so much negligence as upon an infraction of the rule 'sic utere tuo ut alienum non laedas.' I agree, however, that this does not solve the question before us....As I understand the law each person in this country is entitled to bring on his land any quantity of game which can reasonably and properly be kept on it, and so that nothing extraordinary and non-natural is done....So here, so long as the lessee of the right of shooting was exercising the ordinary rights which the landlord who had reserved the right might have exercised, he was acting within his rights, but the moment he brings on game to an unreasonable amount or causes it to increase to an unreasonable extent, he is doing that which is unlawful, and an action may be maintained by his neighbour for the damage which he has sustained."

It is to be noticed that the remarks of Pollock B. as far as the occupier of the land is concerned and apart from contract, are obiter dicta merely.

Apparently there has been no actual decision on the main question. As in Farrer v. Nelson so in Hilton v. Green ([1862], 2 F. & F. 821), Birkbeck v. Paget ([1862], 31 Beav. 403) and Paget v. Birkbeck ([1863], 3 F. & F. 683) the question was the liability to the occupier of the land of a person entitled to the right of shooting over that occupier's land, not his liability to an adjoining owner.

In such cases the question to be determined is whether the act of bringing the animals on the land is authorised by the right granted to the defendant. The question of the rights of adjoining owners or occupiers is quite a different matter and does not depend on grant. The maxim "sic utere" etc. does not contribute much towards a solution of the question. As Erle J. points out (El. Bl. & El. 643) "The maxim is mere verbiage; a party may damage property

of another where the law permits, and he may not
where the law prohibits, so that the maxim cannot be
applied till the law is ascertained, and when it is the
maxim is superfluous." It is also a question of much
difficulty as to what is comprised in the term "animal"
in the passage quoted from the judgment of Pollock B.

The matter was again considered in Brady v.
Warren ([1900] 2 Ir. Rep. 632), and discussed in great
detail, but there was no necessity for a decision on
the point. However, it was there said: "In order
to maintain the present action it is not sufficient for
the plaintiff to show that he has sustained damage
by wild rabbits which came from defendant's demesne;
he must also show that such damage was caused by
defendant's going beyond what was reasonably necessary in order to enable him to have the natural and
reasonable use and enjoyment of his own land which
is his lawful right. If the plaintiff only shows that his
land is damaged by defendant using his land in the
natural manner he cannot succeed. At the present time
it is not unlawful or unnatural or unreasonable use of
land for the owner to have on it ground or feathered
game or rabbits all wild by nature, to such a moderate
extent as the land is so circumstanced as to be reasonably capable of supporting; and if pursuing their
natural instincts the ground game or rabbits stray or
winged game fly to neighbouring land, the neighbour,
though he sustain damage by such game or rabbits,
has not I think a right of action against the owner
of the land from which such game or rabbits stray or
fly; because, being wild by nature he has no property
in them, and the neighbour may himself acquire the

property in them by reducing them into possession on his land, and then it is his game or rabbits....It may be that the case would be different if the damage of which the plaintiff complains was caused by the defendant actively doing anything going beyond what is reasonable to enable him to have the natural use and enjoyment of his own land such as bringing or collecting or preserving (which is equivalent to collecting) game wild by nature ferae naturae, ground or feathered, on his land to an immoderate extent beyond what the land is reasonably capable of supporting—overburdening, or, as it is commonly expressed, overstocking his land with game which must in that case, in the nature of things, seek for sustenance or shelter elsewhere" (Johnson J.). At the trial of the action the jury had been directed that they must be satisfied that there was a use of the rabbits by the defendant as his property which would impose a duty of reasonable care not to injure his neighbour in the mode of using his own property. On appeal, Johnson J. does not seem to have taken a different view as to the ground of liability, but he held in the particular case that the rabbits were not the rabbits of the defendant, nor his property, nor kept by him; but were wild rabbits, animals ferae naturae, for whose acts defendant was not responsible.

The fact that such a nuisance exists does not justify a trespass by an adjoining landowner in order to abate it. Moreover, a claim by a commoner to fill up burrows and to destroy rabbits which are kept in such numbers as to be a surcharge of the common cannot be upheld. The proper remedy in such a case

is by action at law. "A coney burrow is not, of its
own nature, a nuisance: on the contrary, it is essential
to a free warren. Therefore the nuisance depends
upon the number of them, and you can, at the utmost,
only abate so much of the thing as is a nuisance. You
cannot destroy the whole (which is the right here
claimed) but only so much of the thing as makes it a
nuisance." (Cooper v. Marshall [1757], 1 Burr. 259.)

SECTION II. *By reclaimed animals*

1. **The person who tames or reclaims an
animal which is usually found in a wild state
in this country is liable for any trespass
committed by it and for the natural and
ordinary consequences of such trespass.**

The person who takes and tames or reclaims an
animal ferae naturae acquires a qualified property in
the animal. At the same time and by reason of his
right of property he accepts responsibility if it escapes
and trespasses on the land of another. The rule with
regard to animals ferae naturae which have been
reduced into possession and tamed or reclaimed is the
same, therefore, as that obtaining in the case of
domestic animals, namely, that their owner is liable,
when they escape and trespass, for any damage caused
by them, provided that such damage is the natural
and ordinary consequence of such trespass.

Therefore where tame pigeons or doves destroy
another's crops, an action will lie for the damage caused

by them. (Dewell v. Saunders [1618], Cro. Jac. 490.)
Here it was held (disapproving of a resolution to the
contrary in Boulston v. Hardy) that the erecting of
a new pigeon-house by the freeholder of a manor is
not a common nuisance inquirable at the leet. "But
Montague said if those who have not any lands at all
should erect dove-houses, and increase multitude of
pigeons, to the grievance of the country, it may be
enquired of before the justices of Assize." The
reporter also adds the following: "Note that in the
argument of this case Justice Doderidge said that if
pigeons come upon my land I may kill them, and the
owner hath not any remedy; but the owner of the
land is to take heed that he take them not by any mean
prohibited by the statutes: to which opinion Croke
and Houghton accorded. But Montague held ˌ the
contrary and that the party hath jus proprietatis in
them, for they are as domestics and have animum
revertendi and ought not to be killed; and for the
killing of them an action lies: but the other opinion is
the best."

Deer, though animals ferae naturae, may be
reclaimed and belong to the person who has tamed
them so as to make him responsible for trespass by
them and the ordinary consequences of such trespass.
In the case of Brady v. Warren ([1900] 2 Ir. Rep. 632)
deer had been confined in a walled deer-park on
defendant's estate. Several years prior to defendant's
coming into possession of the estate, a portion of the
surrounding wall had been blown down and a number
of deer had escaped. The wall was repaired, and
although further dilapidations occurred from time to

time, apparently no other deer got out. The deer
which had escaped wandered about the estate and
began to trespass on plaintiff's farm which adjoined
the estate, causing great damage to his crops. After
defendant came into possession, the trespasses became
more frequent, but the animals always returned to
the estate. Defendant organised parties to shoot the
deer which roamed the estate, gave permission to the
plaintiff to shoot the deer, and announced generally
that anyone who could shoot them might do so. He,
however, kept a woodranger to look after the deer,
and this man had seen deer wandering some distance
from the estate but was unable to say whether they
returned. Moreover, defendant's predecessor had been
used to feed the animals in winter with hay, laurel and
oats, but defendant had not continued the practice.
On these facts it was held by a majority of the Court
that there was evidence to support the finding of
the jury that the deer were defendant's deer, that
they were tame and domesticated, and were "kept"
by defendant and under his control; and that the
defendant was liable for any damage done by the deer
to plaintiff's land and crops.

Bees are reclaimed and become the subject of
property when they are hived, but it is questionable
whether the person who hives them becomes responsible in law if in the ordinary course of their activities
they fly to adjoining lands and there sting cattle or
human beings. Such would not seem to be a natural
and probable consequence of their escape. (O'Gorman
v. O'Gorman [1903] 2 Ir. Rep. 573.)

It is unnecessary to give further illustrations of

this part of the subject here, as the rules are worked out in greater detail when dealing with the trespass of domestic animals.

2. The responsibility for the trespass of tamed or reclaimed animals ceases when they have reverted to their wild state. Whether such animals have so reverted is a question of fact in each case.

"If one kept a tame fox which gets loose and grows wild, he that kept him before shall not answer for the damage the fox doth after he hath lost him and he hath remained in his wild nature." (Opinion of Marsden J. Anon. 1 Ventr. 295.)

Though this opinion is doubted by Johnson J. in Brady v. Warren (ante p. 25) and, it may be, with reason in the case of injuries by a fox (if such a case be conceivable), yet logically, and if confined to the case of trespasses by harmless animals, it would seem to be correct in principle. If it be law that a man is not responsible for the trespass of animals ferae naturae, the position follows immediately. For a reclaimed animal is nevertheless an animal ferae naturae although it has lost its wild habits for a time (see Besozzi v. Harris [1858], 1 F. & F. 92). If it regains its wild nature, upon what principle can responsibility for its trespass be attributed to the person who formerly kept it?

Our law follows the Civil law thus far. A divergence between the two is to be noted hereafter in the case of injury caused by a wild animal which has by nature dangerous or mischievous proclivities. And it is probably this case which Johnson J. had in mind when he expressed doubts as to the correctness of the opinion of Marsden J.

For a fuller illustration of the rule reference must be made to the case of Brady v. Warren (ante p. 25), where it was admitted by defendant that he would be answerable for damage done by escaped deer if they were still to be reckoned as tamed or reclaimed and had not in fact reverted to their wild state.

SECTION III. *By animals domitae naturae*

1. **The owner of domestic animals is bound at his peril to keep his animals from straying on the lands of others. Whether the escape of the animals is due to negligence is immaterial in determining liability.**

With regard to domestic animals the law is clear enough. Their owner is bound at his peril to prevent his animals from straying. "Ils ont fait tort quand les bestes vont oustre la terre." (Y.B. 7 Hen. VII, Mchas. fo. 16, pl. 1.)[1]

The duty is absolute and not one of taking care.

From the early authorities it would seem to be doubtful whether the liability of the owner is trespass or negligence. For instance, Sir William Blackstone in his Commentaries, III. Ch. 12, says that "a man is

[1] Quoted in Prof. Courtney Kenny's *Select Cases on the Law of Torts*, p. 597.

answerable for not only his own *trespass*, but that of his cattle also; for, if by his *negligent keeping* they stray upon the land of another (and much more if he permits, or drives them on) and they there tread down his neighbour's herbage, and spoil his corn or his trees, this is a trespass for which the owner must answer in damages."

At an early date the ground of liability seems to have been further confused by the cases where the harm is suffered through the omission to keep or maintain a fence in repair. Cases of this nature are almost always concerned with the escape and trespass of animals, although the principles governing the two matters are quite distinct.

The owners of adjoining closes are, at common law, not bound to fence either against or for the benefit of each other. (Star v. Rookesby [1711], 1 Salk. 335, Churchill v. Evans [1809], 1 Taunt. 529, Hilton v. Ankesson [1872], 27 L.T. 519.) But an owner of land may be bound by statute, agreement or prescription to fence his land for the benefit of an adjoining occupier. Prescription is by far the most usual source of the obligation, which has been said to be "in the nature of a spurious easement" affecting the land of the person who is bound to maintain the fence.

Although the nature of the prescriptive obligation in early law was not certain, in modern law the maintenance of the fence, where it is enjoined, is an absolute duty which may be violated by simple omission on the part of the person upon whom that duty is cast, whether plaintiff or defendant. It follows that the omission to repair the fence may be urged as matter of defence, or it may be adopted as the foundation of liability. And it occurs in connection with (*a*) damage caused by trespassing animals, or (*b*) harm caused to animals whilst straying. Thus in an old case reported in 1 Ventr. 264 the action was in case "in defectu fensurarum" for the loss of a mare which had been drowned in a ditch on defendants' land, having escaped there through a gap in a hedge which defendants were prescriptively bound to maintain.

The two grounds of liability and the reasons for them are stated in the case of Star v. Rookesby ([1711], 1 Salk. 335). "Error was brought on a judgment by default in C.B. in an action on the case, wherein the plaintiff declared that he was possessed of a close adjoining to the defendant's, and that the tenants and occupiers of that close had time out of mind made and repaired the fence between the plaintiff's and defendant's close, and that for want of repair the defendant's cattle came into the plaintiff's close, etc. Et per cur.: First, Either trespass or case lies; trespass, because it was the plaintiff's ground and not the defendant's; and case, because the first wrong was a nonfeasance and neglect to repair, and that omission is the gist of the action; and the trespass is only consequential damage."

By the writ "de curia claudenda" the person entitled by prescription to the benefit of the fence could compel the adjoining owner to keep the fence in repair and, at the same time, recover damages for the consequences of its non-repair.

A modern instance of the nature of the obligation is given in the case of Lawrence v. Jenkins ([1873],

L.R. 8 Q.B. 274). Defendant, who was the occupier
of a close adjoining another close occupied by plaintiff,
sold the timber on his close to a third person who cut
down a tree in such a negligent manner as to break a
gap in the hedge dividing the two closes. Two cows
belonging to plaintiff got through this gap and ate
some yew leaves in defendant's close, with the result
that the animals were poisoned and died. The
evidence showed that defendant and his predecessors
had for more than forty years repaired the fence which
was on his land, and that for the last nineteen years
the fence had been repaired by defendant and his
predecessors upon notice by the occupier for the time
being of plaintiff's close. Whenever repairs were
executed they were for the purpose of preventing
cattle on plaintiff's close from escaping into defendant's
close. The Court came to the conclusion upon the
evidence that the defendant was bound at his peril
to maintain at all times, and without notice to repair
it, a sufficient fence; and that except in the case of
damage by the act of God, or vis major, he would be
answerable for damage sustained by cattle escaping
from the plaintiff's close by reason of the defective
state of the fence, and proximately due to that cause.

The fact that plaintiff was a gratuitous bailee of
the animal makes no difference. (Rooth v. Wilson [1817],
1 B. & Ald. 59.) The defendant is liable for all the
natural consequences of his omission to repair the
fence, but not for damage caused by vis major or the
act of God. (Powell v. Salisbury [1828], 2 Y. & J. 391.)
Apart from statute, agreement or prescription it is
now well settled law that there is no duty to erect or

maintain a fence between two adjoining closes, but that even in the absence of such a duty the owner of animals is bound to prevent them straying. "There can be no doubt that the general rule of law is that a man is only bound to take care that his cattle do not wander from his own land and trespass upon the lands of others." (Bayley J. in Boyle v. Tamlyn [1827], 6 B. & C. 337.) "At common law the owners of adjoining closes are not bound to fence either against or for the benefit of each other; but in the absence of fences each owner is bound to prevent his cattle or other animals from trespassing on his neighbour's premises." (Archibald J. in Lawrence v. Jenkins, supra.) See also Churchill v. Evans ([1809], 1 Taunt. 529) and Tenant v. Goldwin ([1704], 6 Mod. 314). The same views are expressed by Coleridge L.C.J. in the case of Ellis v. Loftus Iron Co. ([1874], L.R. 10 C.P. 10), and by Stephen J. in Tillett v. Ward ([1882], 10 Q.B.D. 19), both of which cases there will be occasion to mention in detail in another connection.

Similarly there is no general rule of law imposing the obligation on the owner or occupier of lands abutting on a public road to keep up the fences separating the close from the road. (Potter v. Parry [1859], 7 W.R. 182; Binks v. South Yorkshire Railway and River Dun Company [1862], 3 B. & S. 244.) This has an important bearing on the law dealing with the straying of animals from private property upon a public highway where they do acts of harm. This matter will be dealt with later.

What is said to be the modern view as to the liability is stated by Mr Justice Brett (in L.R.

2 C.P. 10) as follows: "Having looked into the
authorities it appears to me that the result of them is
that in the case of animals trespassing on land the
mere act of the animal belonging to a man, which he
could not. foresee, or which he took all reasonable
means of preventing, may be a trespass, inasmuch as
the same act, if done by himself, would have been a
trespass[1]." If this view is the correct one, it at least
must not be taken in any way to be inconsistent with
the next rule as to remoteness of damage, the principle
of which is well-settled law.

The law seems to take a laxer view of the responsibility for trespass in the case of dogs than in the case
of other domestic animals. In an old case, Millen v.
Fawdrey ([1625], as reported in Latch. 119), Littleton J.
said: "Et est un difference inter un chein & auters
avers; si un chein vaer en vostre terre naveres action."
And the reason he gives is that "ley ne presumer, que
home avera tiel command sur son chein a recaller luy
al instant."

In a later and better known case of Mason v. Keeling
([1700], 1 Ld Raym. 606), Holt C.J. said: "...there is
a great difference between horses and oxen, in which a
man has a valuable property, and which are not so
familiar to mankind, and dogs; the former the owner
ought to confine, and take all reasonable caution, that
they do no mischief, otherwise an action will lie against
him; but otherwise of dogs, before he has notice of
some mischievous quality....And the law does not
oblige the owner to keep the dog in his house; for if
the dog break a neighbour's close, the owner will not

---

[1] Quoted in Pollock's *Law of Torts*, 6th Edn,   479.

be subject to an action for it. But if a servant leaves
open the stable door, and a coach-horse runs out and
does mischief, it is otherwise."

The true meaning of Lord Holt's words has been
the subject of much conjecture. In Cox v. Burbidge
([1863], 13 C.B. (N.S.) 430) Willes J. gives what he
thinks is the origin for the distinction drawn between
dogs and other domestic animals, and is of opinion
that "control" is meant by Lord Holt instead of
"property." "I can quite understand a distinction
being drawn between animals which from their natural
tendency to stray, and thereby to do real damage,
require to be and usually are restrained, and a dog
which is not usually kept confined; and there may be
good reason besides 'de minimis non curat lex' why
an action should not lie against a man whose dog
without the will of its master enters another's land,
though it is different in the case of a horse or an ox.
Perhaps control was meant by Lord Holt and not
property. His dictum exhausts itself on the liability
of the owners of horses and oxen for trespasses committed by them on land, pursuing their ordinary
instincts in search of food."

In the case of Brown v. Giles ([1823], 1 C. & P. 118),
Park J. thought that the case of a dog jumping into a
field, without the consent of its master, not only was
not a wilful trespass, but was no trespass at all on
which an action could be maintained.

The reasons which have been offered for a distinction in this respect between dogs on the one hand
and oxen on the other were stated in Read v. Edwards
([1864], 17 C.B. (N.S.) 245) to be first, the difficulty or

impossibility of keeping the former under restraint; secondly, the slightness of the damage which their wandering ordinarily causes; thirdly, the common usage of mankind to allow them a wider liberty; and, lastly, their not being considered at common law so absolutely the chattels of their owner, as to be the subject of larceny. The question whether such a distinction did exist was not actually decided in that case because the action was not for a mere trespass but for chasing and destroying game, and it was proved at the trial that the dog which did the damage was of a peculiarly mischievous disposition, was to the knowledge of its owner accustomed to chase and destroy game, and, notwithstanding this, was allowed to roam at large in the vicinity of plaintiff's wood in which there was game.

In Sanders v. Teape and Swan ([1884], 51 L.T. 263), a dog, which was being taken out by one of the defendants, in running about in playfulness, jumped over a low wall and fell on the plaintiff who was working in a stooping posture in a hole on the other side of the wall. In an action for damages for the injuries sustained it was held that, inasmuch as the dog was not shown to be mischievous to the knowledge of the owner, the plaintiff had no cause of action either as for a trespass or as for any breach of duty. "If a man keeps horses and other animals, he is bound to keep them on his own ground; if he does not he may be liable to an action of trespass. There is an exception to this when they are on a public highway, as they have a right to be there, and then the owner is bound to use ordinary care. But in the case of dogs, pigeons and the like,

3—2

the case is different; if a dog, not being exceptionally mischievous, acting in playfulness goes over another man's land, there is no trespass, and the owner of the dog would not be liable. Here, so far as the defendants are concerned, the occurrence was purely accidental and involuntary" (Williams J.). The last words seem to give the key to the whole question. Such trespasses on the part of animals which are usually allowed full liberty are involuntary trespasses and fall under the general exceptions from liability in tort which are usually classed under the heading of inevitable accident.

2. Although the duty is absolute to prevent animals from straying upon the property of others, yet the liability resulting from a breach of that duty extends only to the natural and probable consequences of the wrong and not to remote consequences.

This qualification of the general rule is not in any way exceptional, but merely an instance of the application of the general principles of liability in tort. "When complaint is made that one person has caused harm to another, the first question is whether his act (or default) was really the 'cause' of that harm in a sense upon which the law can take action. The harm or loss may be traceable to his act, but the connection may be, in the accustomed phrase, too remote.... The distinction of proximate from remote consequences is needful, first to ascertain whether there is any liability at all, and then, if it is established that wrong has been committed, to settle the footing on which compensation for the wrong is to be awarded[1]." In the majority of cases of liability for tort, and especially in cases of negligence, the two functions are inseparable. The very process which determines the question of liability at the same time ascertains the consequences of the wrong of which the law can take notice. To this, violations of absolute duties are an exception. There, remoteness of damage is material, not to found liability, but merely to ascertain the extent of responsibility when established. Here we are dealing with the case of an absolute duty, that of preventing one's animals from straying. Trespass is an actionable wrong in itself. "Every invasion of private property, be it ever so minute, is a trespass." (Entick v. Carrington [1765], 19 St. Tr. 1029.) And every trespass is said to import a damage. Therefore an action will lie for the trespass of an animal irrespective of the extent of the trespass or the amount of the damage done. Some harm, if only nominal, is always presumed. (Ellis v. Loftus Iron Co. [1874], L.R. 10 C.P. 10.) But on the one hand, "de minimis non curat lex," and on the other, some of the consequences of the wrong may be altogether too remote. It is therefore material to enquire whether the harm suffered was or was not too remote in order to settle for what consequences of the owner's act or default compensation is to be awarded. It is apprehended that those consequences are not too remote which the owner of the animal might have expected to result from its straying on the land of another.

---

[1] See Pollock's *Law of Torts*, 6th Edn, p. 28 *et seq.*, where the matter is discussed in detail.

The following extract from the judgment of Williams J. in Cox v. Burbidge ([1863], 13 C.B. (N.S.) 430), itself an action for negligence, gives us a clear statement of the law with regard to the trespass of animals to the land of others and the measure of the consequences for which the owner is held answerable.

"If I am the owner of an animal in which by law the right of property can exist, I am bound to take care that it does not stray into the land of my neighbour; and I am liable for any trespass it may commit and for the ordinary consequences of that trespass. Whether or not the escape of the animal is due to my negligence, is altogether immaterial. I am clearly liable for the trespass, and for all the ordinary consequences of the trespass, subject to a distinction which is taken very early in the books that the animal is such that the owner of it may have a property in it which is recognisable by law. For instance, if a man's cattle or sheep or poultry stray into his neighbour's land or garden, and do such damage as might ordinarily be expected to be done by things of that sort, the owner is liable to his neighbour for the consequences."

The rule as to remoteness of damage has been worked out only gradually and by particular cases.

In Lee v. Riley ([1865], 18 C.B. (N.S.) 722) it was established that the natural consequences of the trespass may include even harm caused by a spontaneous act of the animal. Through defect in fences which it was defendant's duty to repair, his mare strayed during the night from his close into an adjoining field and so into a field of the plaintiff's in which was a horse. From some unexplained cause, the animals quarrelled, and the result was that plaintiff's horse received a kick from the defendant's mare which broke the leg of the horse and necessitated its being killed. The Court of Common Pleas held upon these facts that the defendant was responsible for his mare's trespass and that the damage was not too remote. Erle C.J. said: "It is plain that the defendant's mare was trespassing on the plaintiff's close; and I think it equally clear upon the evidence that the defendant's mare did inflict upon the plaintiff's horse the injury which was the cause of its death; the question is, whether or not the damage was too remote. The contest at the trial seems to have been whether or not the mare was of a ferocious or vicious disposition, and whether the defendant knew it. But I think it was not necessary to go into that question because the act which upon the evidence must be presumed to have caused the injury was not one which was characteristic of vice or ferocity in the mare in the ordinary sense.... I think there was abundant evidence to warrant the jury in coming to the conclusion that the defendant's mare did trespass on the plaintiff's close, and there did the injury of which the plaintiff complained." Montague Smith J. adopted the omission to keep up the fence as the ground of action but was even more explicit in the view that the damage was not too remote. "The only question is whether or not the injury so caused was too remote. It was contended that it was, because the plaintiff gave no proof that the defendant's mare was vicious, and that the defendant knew it. I do not think it was necessary to give any such evidence. The accident might have happened

without any vice in the mare; it might have been
and probably was occasioned by the sudden meeting
together of strange horses in the night-time. If even
the plaintiff's horse committed the first assault the
defendant would under the circumstances I think have
been equally liable."

Although the actual trespass be trivial, yet if it be
established, the owner will be liable for the natural
consequences however disproportionate to the trespass
they may seem to be. In Ellis v. Loftus Iron Co.
([1874], L.R. 10 C.P. 10) the plaintiff was the occupier
of a field, a portion of which was, by arrangement, let
to the defendants and fenced in by a wire fencing.
Defendants' entire horse when turned into their plot
bit and kicked plaintiff's mare through the fence. It
was proved that defendants' horse did not cross
the fence, but that both animals were close to the
fence when the injury happened. It was also stated
that the horse was a quiet tempered animal. Lord
Coleridge C.J. in delivering judgment for the plaintiff
in the Court of Common Pleas said: "The judgment
of the County Court Judge must, I think, be reversed,
on the ground that there was evidence of a trespass,
and the damages were not too remote. I cannot say
I entertain any doubt on the matter. It is clear that,
in determining the question of trespass or no trespass,
the Court cannot measure the amount of the alleged
trespass; if the defendant place a part of his foot on
the plaintiff's land unlawfully, it is in law as much a
trespass as if he had walked half a mile on it. It has,
moreover, been held, again and again, that there is a
duty on a man to keep his cattle in, and if they

get on another's land it is a trespass; and that is
irrespective of any question of negligence whether
great or small. In this case it is found that there was
an iron fence on the plaintiff's land, and that the
horse of the defendants did damage to that of the
plaintiff through the fence. It seems to me sufficiently
clear that some portion of the defendants' horse's
body must have been over the boundary. That may
be a very small trespass, but it is a trespass in law.
The only remaining question is, whether the damages
were too remote? I cannot see that they were; they
were the natural and direct consequence of the trespass
committed." But it is not a natural and probable
consequence of allowing a horse to stray unattended
in a highway that it should kick a child who happened
to be playing there. (Cox v. Burbidge [1863], 13 C.B.
(N.S.) 430.) Though the action in this case was in
form an action for negligence, yet such a consequence
has always been held too remote in the case of a
trespassing horse.

In Bradley v. Wallaces ([1913], 82 L.J. (K.B.) 1074),
a workman in the course of his duty was crossing
his employers' yard when he was kicked by a horse
which was standing unattended in the yard. The
horse belonged to another firm whose man had left it
standing whilst he helped their carter with his dray.
The horse was not known by its owners to be vicious.
The kick proved fatal and the dependants of the
workman claimed compensation from his employers
under the Workmen's Compensation Act 1906. The
employers admitted liability but claimed to be indem-
nified under the provisions of Section 6 of the Act

by the owners of the horse. The Court of Appeal held
that even if the horse were trespassing in the yard it
was not an ordinary consequence of the trespass that
the horse should kick the workman. The damage was
too remote and the owners of the horse were not liable.
"It is not in the ordinary course of things that a
horse, not known to be vicious, should kick a man.
So far as trespass is concerned, if a horse, pursuant to
its natural instincts, eats a neighbour's hay, or in any
other respects indulges its ordinary natural instincts, the
owner may be liable, but otherwise not. The damage
in the present case does not naturally flow from the
trespass, and is not an ordinary consequence of the
trespass. It is too remote" (per Cozens-Hardy M.R.).

It is submitted that the doctrine of scienter (which
will be fully dealt with hereafter) as such has no true
application in cases of this sort. Whether the animal
was vicious and whether the owner knew it, the
question resolves itself solely into one of remoteness
of damage. With regard to the case of injuries to
human beings, the limits of liability seem to be the
same whether the ground of action is trespass, negligence or a breach of the absolute duty. But this
would seem to be only accidental, and it is doubtful
whether the liability in trespass and the liability under
the absolute duty exactly coincide in every case. It
will be necessary to refer to this matter in another
place of this work.

One writer, citing the cases of Lee v. Riley ([1865],
18 C.B. (N.S.) 722) and Ellis v. Loftus Iron Co. ([1874],
L.R. 10 C.P. 10) puts the law in this way: "Where
an animal is a trespasser, it is immaterial that an injury

done by it is due to the animal's vice. The owner in such case is liable for all the damage it may do, whether the damage is such as may reasonably be expected from the nature of the animal or is due to mischievous propensities of which the owner is ignorant." (Addison on the *Law of Torts*, 6th Edn, p. 129.) With deference, it is submitted that this is rather a misleading statement. It would lead one to suppose that the liability extended even to remote consequences, which is certainly not the case. Thus in the case of Bradley v. Wallaces, just quoted, Kennedy L.J. said: "The learned County Court Judge, if, as I hope, I follow his line of reasoning, seems to have thought that, directly you have a horse in a position which renders its owner constructively a trespasser, every damage done in any way by the horse to any person or to the property of any one is an actionable wrong. I venture to think that such is not, and never was, the law." In the same case Swinfen Eady L.J. generalises the rule in these terms: "The guiding principle is that a person is liable only for the natural and probable consequences occasioned by or resulting from trespass, or negligence; an injury suffered must be brought within this degree to give rise to a cause of action."

In certain cases the common law adopted an exceptionally stringent rule of responsibility for wrongs resulting from acts (not necessarily wrongful) exposing the person or property of others to extraordinary risk of harm. The duty imposed in such cases was not merely a duty of using reasonable care and caution, but an absolute duty of insuring others against resulting harm; at any rate, so long as such harm was not due to a cause altogether beyond human foresight and control. The mere fact of the harm having happened gave rise to a liability which was not capable of being avoided by showing that even a degree of diligence proportioned to the exigencies of the case 'had been observed. For instance, the possessor of loaded firearms, explosives, or poisons; the person who kindled fire in an unusual place or for an extraordinary purpose; the person who brought on his land and kept there anything likely to do mischief if it escaped, must be prepared to be answerable to others for any damage which resulted, within the limits before indicated. No satisfactory evidence in support of any of the theories as to the origin of the rule has as yet been advanced. But it seems tolerably certain that in the Anglo-Saxon law this duty of insurance, instead of being exceptional, was the general legal doctrine at the basis of all liability in tort. The policy of the adoption of such a stringent rule, or at any rate of its retention in modern times in the few cases in which it does exist, has been the subject also of much discussion; but the matter is outside the scope of this present work[1].

In modern times the general principles of liability have undergone a great modification, and the cases of strict responsibility now remaining are so difficult to piece into the modern legal system that they themselves are in the highest degree exceptional. Cattle-trespass is probably the oldest instance of this strict liability.

---

[1] For a discussion of these exceptional cases see Pollock's *Law of Torts*, 6th Edn, Ch. XII.

Under the early practice, damage caused by straying cattle was remediable in an action of trespass. Now the action of trespass was the appropriate remedy for direct and forcible injuries either to the person or to property. Forcible injuries are those due to physical interference or contact. Direct injuries are such as follow immediately upon the act of the wrongdoer. Injuries which, by reason of some intervening circumstance, cannot be regarded as part of the defendant's act are said to be "consequential injuries." Redress for injuries which were either not forcible or not direct but consequential had to be sought in an action of trespass on the case, more shortly termed "case," or "an action on the case." The question whether trespass or case lay, did not depend on whether the injury was intentional or accidental. If the injury were direct and forcible, trespass was the proper remedy, whether the injury was the result of intention or negligence. If the injury were consequential, case was the remedy even if the injury was intended. In certain cases either remedy was available, that is to say, where the same act produced both a direct and a consequential injury. Here the plaintiff might have an action of trespass alleging the consequential injury as special damage, or he might waive the trespass and take his remedy in case for the consequential injury alone. "Trespass for the entry of diseased cattle into the plaintiff's close per quod the plaintiff's cattle were infected. Not guilty pleaded, and a verdict for the plaintiff for 20*s*. It was moved to allow the plaintiff his full costs, upon the account of the special damages alleged and put in issue, and which would have subsisted of itself as a distinct cause of action, and the plaintiff ought not to be punished for joining it with the trespass, to avoid vexation. And Cro. Car. 163, 307, 3 Mod. 39, 2 Ventr. 48, Cro. Car. 141, Ray 487 were cited. On the other side it was insisted, that though here is matter of aggravation laid yet it is still to be considered as an action of trespass, in which there is a recovery under 40s. And matter alleged only by way of aggravation cannot intitle the plaintiff to full costs (2 Ventr. 48, Salk. 642). The Chief Justice, Powys and Fortescue Justices, were for full costs, because the consequential damage is a matter for which the plaintiff might have had a distinct satisfaction. And they likened it to the case of an action of battery, per quod consortium of the wife, or servitium of the servant amisit, which for that reason are not within the statute[1]. The true distinction is, where the matter alleged by way of aggravation will intitle the party to a distinct satisfaction. Asportation of trees may be a ground for a trover, but yet may be laid as an aggravation in trespass, and the plaintiff shall have full costs. If a man enters and chases and kills my cattle, that is a distinct wrong, but yet may be joined as matter of aggravation. Suppose I have two closes at a great distance, and the same water-course running through both, I may allege the entry into one, per quod the water was prevented from coming to the other, and there shall be full costs. Eyre J. contra. Because this recovery will not be pleadable to a special action upon the case for the special injury, quod caeteri negaverunt. And the plaintiff had full costs."

---

[1] *Semble* 22 and 23 Car. II, c. 9.

(Anderson v. Buckton [1719], 1 Str. 192[1].) The distinction between the two forms of action was important. The wrong which was remediable in trespass was actionable per se, i.e. without proof of damage. A nuisance or other wrong actionable only on proof of damage was the subject of an action on the case.

Bearing the above explanations in mind, if a person drives cattle on the land of another, this being a forcible and direct injury is remediable in trespass. But if by reason of insufficient fencing or watching, cattle stray on the land of another and do damage, this, being a consequential injury merely, is remediable in case, strictly speaking. But this is just where the actual practice differed. Though it would seem to be an anomaly, yet, under the old practice, cases of the latter sort were remediable in trespass.

That the general rules of the law of trespass are applicable to the cases of straying cattle is substantiated by the following considerations. First, there seems to be no doubt that cattle trespass is actionable per se. (Ellis v. Loftus Iron Co. [1874], L.R. 10 C.P. 10, ante, p. 40.) Secondly, the liability extends only to the trespass of cattle and other animals in which at common law a right of property could exist, and such a condition was a sine qua non of the remedy in an action of trespass. However this may be, the material point is that trespass was in practice the appropriate form of action, and the reason possibly was that the wrong is not akin to nuisance, which ground seems to underlie most of the few other cases of strict responsi-

---

[1] This case was disapproved in Daubney v. Cooper ([1830], 10 B. C. 831) though only as to the question of costs.

bility at the present day remaining in our law. These cases of absolute liability are said to have received their generalisation in the case of Rylands v. Fletcher ([1868], L.R. 3 H.L. 330), where the House of Lords affirmed and adopted a judgment of the Exchequer Chamber in these terms: "We think that the true rule of law is, that the person who, for his own purposes, brings on his land and collects and keeps there anything likely to do mischief if it escapes, must keep it in at his peril; and if he does not do so, is prima facie answerable for all the damage which is the natural consequence of its escape. He can excuse himself by showing that the escape was owing to the plaintiff's default; or perhaps that the escape was the consequence of vis major, or the act of God.... The person whose grass or corn is beaten down by the escaping cattle of his neighbour, or whose mine is flooded by the water from his neighbour's reservoir, or whose cellar is invaded by the filth of his neighbour's privy, or whose habitation is made unhealthy by the fumes and noisome vapours of his neighbour's alkali works, is damnified without any fault of his own. And it seems but reasonable and just that the neighbour who has brought on his own property something which was not naturally there— harmless to others so long as it is confined to his own property, but which he knows will be mischievous if it gets on his neighbour's—should be obliged to make good the damage which ensues if he does not succeed in confining it to his own property. But for his act in bringing it there, no mischief could have accrued; and it seems but just that he should at his peril keep it there so that no mischief may accrue, or answer for

the natural and anticipated consequence. And upon
authority, this, we think, is established to be the law,
whether the things so brought be beasts, or water, or
filth, or stenches." (L.R. 1 Ex. p. 279.)

The instances recited in the judgment, except that of
escaping cattle, are all wrongs in the nature of a nuisance.
They are instances of the unnatural user of land—of
cases where a person has brought something on his own
property which was not naturally there. How can this
be said of cattle and like animals? What more natural
use can there be of land than to keep cattle upon it?

The foregoing considerations all point to the
conclusion that the so-called "rule in Rylands v.
Fletcher" did not find its source in the original cases
of strict liability of which cattle-trespass was the type.

Section IV. *Exceptions to liability*

Liability for trespass of animals is excluded
where:

(*a*) the trespass is involuntary; or

(*b*) the trespass is due to vis major, or
the act of God; or

(*c*) the trespass is occasioned by the
omission of a third person whose duty it was
to keep a fence in repair and over whom
defendant had no control; or

(*d*) the plaintiff is bound by law to fence out
defendant's cattle and he omits to do so; or

(*e*) the trespass is committed from a highway where the animals are lawfully passing.

Enquiry must now be made as to what exceptions there are to the absolute duty of preventing the escape of animals and their trespass to the lands of others.

And first, in general, no action lies for an "involuntary trespass." This applies not only to the case of animals but to the law of trespass generally, and there is abundance of authority for it. But what constitutes an involuntary trespass in the case of animals is not quite clear. Apparently where the owner of the animal is present and cannot by any reasonable or available means prevent the trespass, no liability attaches to him in law. To be "involuntary" the trespass must occur at a time when the owner of the animal has the opportunity but not the ability to exercise his "voluntas."

An early authority for the exception in the case of animals is the dictum of Catesby J. (in Y.B. 22 Edw. IV, fo. 24): "If a man comes with a drove of cattle on the high road past where trees or corn or other crops are growing, then, should any of the beasts eat from these crops, the man who was driving them would have a good defence, provided the thing happened against his will. For the law understands that a man cannot control his cattle all the while. But if he permitted them, or if he let them continue, then it would be otherwise[1]."

Similarly it is laid down in 2 Rolle Abr. 566, pl. 1, that if cattle, in passage on the highway, eat herbs or corn "raptim et sparsim," against the will of the owner, it will excuse the trespass.

---

[1] Quoted in Prof. Courtney Kenny's *Select Cases on the Law of Torts*, p. 600.

"Millen port action de trespass vers Fawtry pur
enchaser ove un chiene ses barbits al Dale en un close
appell. B. close, le defendant plede en barre que il ad
un estate en Whiteclose en S. parish adjoinant al dit
B. close & que le dit barbits fueront damage fesant en
W. close & il ove un petit chiene enchase le dit barbits
al B. close, & tam cito que il vient a le dit chiene
il luy recall & revoke que fuit mesme le trespass, &
sur ceo le plaintiff demurre en ley. Et cest terme il
fuit resolve per tout le court, scilicet, les 4 justices,
que le action ne gist, car il fuit legal al party per luy
mesme, ou per un chiene a chaser ses barbits hors
de son terre esteant la damage fesant, & coment le
chiene eux enchase en le close d'un auter, tamen
quant il luy recall tam cito que poterit, ceo ne fait
luy trespasser...." (Millen v. Fawtry [1625] Jon. W.
131, Termino Pasch. An. 11 Caroli Regis, in Banco
Regis.) It is the same case apparently which is more
fully reported in Poph. 161, under the title of Mitten v.
Faudrye, an instance of the corruption of case names.
See also Latch. 119, where Littleton J. is reported as
adopting a similar view. In the report of the case in
Popham, Doderidge J. agreed that trespass did not lie
"for here was no hedge, and when he saw them out of
his own ground, he rated the dog,...and the nature of
a dog is such that he can not be ruled suddenly, and
here it appeareth to be an involuntary trespass. A
man is driving goods through a town, and one of them
goes into another man's house, and he follows him,
trespass doth not lie for this, because it was involuntary,
and a trespass ought to be done voluntarily, and so
it is injuria, and a hurt to another, and so it is damnum."

4—2

The same principle was applied in the case of Beckwith v. Shoredike ([1767], 4 Burr. 2092), where it was laid down that "if A goes along a footpath, and his dog happens to escape from him and run into a paddock, and pull down a deer against his will, it is no trespass."

Secondly, it seems that the act of God or vis major would be an excuse. The case of Powell v. Salisbury ([1828], 2 Y. & J. 391) is cited by some writers as an authority, but it does not support the exception in any respect; for first, the action there was in case for neglect to repair fences; secondly, the point was taken by counsel in the course of argument only; and thirdly, the case was not one of damage caused by animals. The plaintiff declared in case against the defendant, for not repairing his fences per quod the plaintiff's horses escaped into the defendant's close, and were there killed by the falling of a haystack: held that the damage was not too remote, and that the action was maintainable.

The exception from the general rule was allowed, however, in the judgment of the Exchequer Chamber in Rylands v. Fletcher ([1866], L.R. 1 Exch. 265), and was subsequently acted upon in the decision of the same court in the case of Nichols v. Marsland ([1875], L.R. 10 Ex. 255). But in the latter case the term was not used in its strict sense of "an operation of natural forces so violent and unexpected that no human foresight or skill could possibly have prevented its effects." It was held to be enough that the occurrence should be such as human foresight could not be reasonably expected to anticipate. Whether, in regard to trespass by animals, vis major or the act of God has the extended meaning one cannot say, as there appears to be no case directly in point. If, as is submitted, the general rules of liability for trespass are applicable, it would seem to follow that the strict meaning should be given to the term in this connection.

The defendant is not liable where the trespass was occasioned by the omission of a third person whose duty it was to keep the fences in repair and over whom defendant had no control. Thus in Wiseman v. Booker ([1878], 3 C.P.D. 184) a railway company let surplus land to the plaintiff, separating it from the adjoining land not taken by means of an open fence four feet high. The plaintiff planted his land with vegetables and these were damaged by horses kept on the adjoining land of the defendant. It appeared that the fences being insufficient, the horses put their heads through and over them and so were enabled to commit the acts of harm complained of. The railway company were under a statutory obligation to maintain the fences. Lopes J. said: "The action is brought in respect of the defendant's horses straying on lands of the plaintiff and destroying his crops. The answer is that the damage was occasioned by defect of a fence which the defendant was under no liability to make and maintain, but the making and maintenance of which was a duty cast by the Act of Parliament (Railway Clauses Consolidation Act 1845, s. 68) upon the railway company whose tenant the plaintiff may for this purpose be assumed to be. The liability cast upon the company by the Act is very much like the old prescriptive liability to fence." And per Lindley J.: "The plaintiff cannot be in a higher or better position than the railway company. The defendant cannot be made responsible for their breach of duty."

A plea in an action of trespass for injury done by cattle that the plaintiff is bound to fence against the defendant's cattle is a good plea. (Y.B. 19 Hen. VI, 33, pl. 68; Nowel v. Smith, Cro. Eliz. 709. See also Singleton v. Williamson [1861], 31 L.J. (Ex.) 17.)

Where animals stray upon private property from a highway along which they are lawfully passing at the time, their owner is not liable unless it happened through his negligence. This is a well settled rule of law the modern ground for which is public convenience. "There is prima facie a public right to and a public advantage in the use of the highway by the public for the usual purposes of trade and traffic, and if the owner of adjacent land were allowed to leave the same unfenced, and entitled at the same time to make any person driving animals along the highway responsible for their straying on to such lands, the use of the highway would be restricted or rendered onerous by the sweeping liability thus imposed....The principle must be, it would seem, that the landowner who does not choose to protect his land from the road cannot impose a liability so burdensome to the usual and legitimate use of the highway on the owner of animals." (27 Sol. Journ. 81.) Beyond noticing here that the case of cattle straying from a highway is an exception to the general rule of liability for trespass to land, it is not proposed to examine the matter now, but to defer consideration in detail until the question of liability for negligence in the control of animals is discussed (post, p. 147).

PART III

INJURIES TO THE PERSON AND TO OTHER ANIMALS, AND DAMAGE TO GOODS

SECTION I. *The absolute duty*

1. (1) A person who keeps an animal of a notoriously ferocious, dangerous or mischievous species keeps it at his own risk, and is liable for the consequences of any act of harm committed by it.

(2) It is immaterial whether he has been negligent in keeping the animal, whether he knew of its dangerous or mischievous nature, or even whether he had good reason to believe that the particular animal was docile and harmless. Both negligence and knowledge are presumed by the law.

The terms "ferocious, dangerous or mischievous" are intended to cover all kinds of harm. For the sake of brevity, however, in the following pages harmful animals are referred to generally as "dangerous animals" as distinguished from "domestic" or "harmless animals."

The rule above stated is said to be a particular application of the broad principle laid down in Rylands v. Fletcher, namely, that if a man brings upon his land something which would not naturally come upon it, and which is liable to do mischief, being in itself dangerous, he must take care to control it so that it does not do any mischief, and he takes that risk upon himself. "The subject of liability for damage done by dangerous animals is a branch of the law to which that principle has been applied in the same way from the times of Lord Holt and Hale down to the present time.   People must not be wiser than the experience of mankind.   If that experience shows that animals of a particular class are dangerous, even though individual animals of that class may be tamed, yet a man who keeps one of that class does so at his own risk and is responsible for any damage which may be done by it." (Bowen L.J. in Filburn v. The People's Palace, etc. Co. [1890], 59 L.J. (Q.B.) 472.)   The following illustrations suffice to show the strict nature of the liability, though to a certain extent they anticipate the discussion upon liability for harm caused by the keeping of domestic or harmless animals.

1 Hale Pleas of the Crown 430 *b*: "These things seem to be agreeable to law, (1) If the owner have notice of the quality of his beast, and it doth anybody hurt, he is chargeable for an action for it.   (2) Though he have no particular notice, that he did any such thing before, yet if it be a beast, that is ferae naturae, as a lion, a bear, a wolf, yea an ape or monkey, if he get loose and do harm to any person, the owner is liable to an action for the damage, and so I knew it

adjudged in Andrew Baker's case, whose child was bit by a monkey, that broke his chain and got loose. (3) And therefore in case of such a wild beast, or in case of a bull or cow, that doth damage, where the owner knows of it, he must at his peril keep him up safe from doing hurt, for though he use his diligence to keep him up, if he escape and do harm, the owner is liable to answer damages." Here we have a clear opinion that the liability is absolute and that negligence need not be shown.

An equally strong authority is R. v. Huggins ([1730], 2 Ld Raym. 1583) where both civil and criminal responsibility are dealt with. "There is a difference between beasts that are ferae naturae as lions and tygers, which a man must always keep up at his peril; and beasts that are mansuetae naturae, and break through the tameness of their nature, such as oxen and horses. In the latter case, an action lies, if the owner has had notice of the quality of the beast; in the former case an action lies, without such notice. As to the point of felony, if the owner have notice of the mischievous quality of the ox, etc. and he uses all proper diligence to keep him up and he happens to break loose and kill a man, it would be very hard to make the owner guilty of felony. But if through negligence the beast goes abroad after warning or notice of his condition, it is the opinion of Hale, that it is manslaughter in the owner. And if he did purposely let him loose, and wander abroad, with a design to do mischief; nay, though it were but a design to fright people and make sport, and he kills a man; it is murder in the owner."

The duty cast upon the person who keeps a
dangerous animal is absolute. He becomes an insurer
against harm resulting from his act. This does not
seem to have been settled law previously to 1846
when the case of May v. Burdett (9 Q.B. 101) did
something towards clearing up many doubts and
difficulties. Hitherto it had been a question whether
want of due care was not the ground of the action.
A uniform course of pleading had not been adopted.
In some cases, besides breach of an absolute duty,
negligence had been expressly averred in the declaration; on the other hand, precedents of declarations
existed in which the absolute duty alone was treated
as the ground of action. Under the earlier practice,
however, it was usual to draw a separate count averring
negligence in not keeping the animal secured.

The authorities on both sides were collected in
argument and examined by the Court in May v. Burdett,
and a considered judgment was delivered which settled
this particular question once for all. In that case the
declaration stated that the defendant wrongfully kept
a certain monkey "well knowing that the said monkey
was of a mischievous and ferocious nature and was
used and accustomed to attack and bite mankind and
that it was dangerous and improper to allow the said
monkey to be at large and unconfined" and that the
said monkey, while being so kept, did attack and bite
the plaintiff. Upon a verdict for plaintiff and motion
to arrest judgment it was objected that the declaration
was bad because it omitted to aver negligence in
keeping the animal.

The cases cited in argument were almost all cases

of injury by domestic or harmless animals; and in truth, the keeping of a naturally dangerous or ferocious animal appears to have been rarely the subject of consideration by the Courts before this time. It is significant that the Court did not treat this case as one of injury by a dangerous animal, as no comment was made on the fact that the averment of knowledge, or "scienter" as it is technically called, had been included in the statements of the declaration. It was rather assumed than questioned that it was proper to allege the scienter in such a case. Since the decision in Filburn's case (ante, p. 14) the monkey would undoubtedly rank with dangerous animals.

Lord Chief Justice Denman in delivering the judgment of the Court (Denman C.J., Pattison, Coleridge and Wightman J.J.) said: "Whoever keeps an animal accustomed to attack and bite mankind, with knowledge that it is so accustomed, is prima facie liable in an action on the case at the suit of any person attacked and injured by the animal, without any averment of negligence or default in the securing or taking care of it. The gist of the action is the keeping the animal after knowledge of its mischievous propensities.... The conclusion to be drawn from an examination of all the authorities appears to us to be this; that a person keeping a mischievous animal with knowledge of its propensities is bound to keep it secure at his peril, and that, if it does mischief, negligence is presumed, without express averment. The precedents as well as the authorities fully warrant this conclusion. The negligence is in keeping such an animal after notice."

A learned American writer finds nothing in this

language to impose an absolute duty. He says: "the decision in this case seems to be that the keeper of such an animal is prima facie responsible for the injuries done by it, but it is not decided that he may not meet the case by showing that he observed in respect to it proper care." (Cooley, *Torts*, 348.)

The presumption of negligence, if indeed it can be called a presumption at all, is a "praesumptio juris et de jure," that is, one in respect of which no evidence can be given in rebuttal. The so-called presumption amounts to positive proof. The negligence is rather "implied" than "presumed" by the law.

Although the duty of preventing a dangerous animal from causing harm is an absolute duty independent of negligence, yet an action will lie for negligently keeping such an animal so as to cause damage. In Wyatt v. The Rosherville Gardens Company (2 T.L.R. 282) the plaintiff had received injuries from the bite of a bear belonging to the defendants and he sought to recover damages on the ground that the bear had been kept by the defendants in an unsafe and improper cage which was dangerous to the public. The bear was kept at defendants' pleasure-gardens in a cage whose railings in some places were 4½ inches apart. The plaintiff, wishing to see the animal, entered the gallery where the cage was and the bear, putting its paw through the bars, injured the plaintiff's arm. No notice was exhibited to warn persons not to enter the gallery, and the steps up to the entrance had a well-worn appearance. In summing up the case to the jury, Mr Baron Huddleston is reported to have said that if persons chose to keep wild and savage animals—such, for instance, as a bear, a tiger, or a lion—they did so at their own risk and peril; and if any such animal caused injury to anybody, they would be liable for the injuries....In this case it mattered not whether the defendants knew or did not know that this bear was savage—they were equally liable and responsible in either case. This being the state of the law, his Lordship continued, had plaintiff's counsel asked him to decide the case on the law alone, he would have had no hesitation in doing so in his favour; for, in his Lordship's opinion, the question of negligence had nothing whatever to do with the defendants' liability in this case. But to prevent further litigation it was better to dispose of the case upon the facts and he would therefore leave two questions to them—(1) Were the defendants guilty of negligence? (2) If they were, then did the plaintiff, by his own course of conduct, contribute to the accident? The jury found for the plaintiff on both questions and judgment was given accordingly.

In Besozzi v. Harris ([1858], 1 F. & F. 92), another "bear" case, evidence of the tameness of the animal was received, in the circumstances of the case, not by way of answer to liability, but in reduction of damages. In addressing the jury, Crowder J. said: "The statement in the declaration that the defendant knew the bear to be of a fierce nature, must be taken to be proved, as everyone must know that such animals as lions and bears are of a savage nature. For though such nature may sleep for a time; this case shows that it may wake up at any time. A person who keeps such an animal is bound so to keep it that it shall do no damage."

This case marks the halfway stage as to the allegation
of scienter with regard to dangerous animals. In
May v. Burdett, twelve years previously, the allegation
of knowledge was apparently thought to be properly
included in the statements of the declaration. Here is
seen the progress towards the stage where knowledge
is immaterial in the sense that the law presumes it.

The law received its final expression in Filburn's
case (ante, p. 14), the latest of its kind. There it was
held that a person who keeps an animal of a dangerous
class does so at his own risk and is responsible for any
injury done by it, even though individual members
of that class of animals may be tamed. In this case,
at the trial before Day J. the questions whether the
elephant was an animal dangerous to man and whether
it was known to the defendants to be dangerous, were
put to the jury and answered in the negative. But
on appeal the Court thought the first question had been
asked out of extreme caution and that both questions
were immaterial.

Although, as stated above, the rule as to the
liability for wrongs due to the keeping of dangerous
animals, or of animals known to have dangerous
propensities, is said to be an application of the broad
principle laid down in Rylands v. Fletcher, it differs
from this principle both in character and in origin.

It has already been mentioned that there were
certain cases in which the common law adopted an
exceptionally strict rule of liability, and that these
were cases of wrongs resulting from acts (not necessarily
wrongful) which exposed the person or property of

others to an extraordinary risk of harm, and several instances of such cases have been given. It is generally considered that the liability for injuries caused by the keeping of animals falls within this class of cases.

The case of Rylands v. Fletcher (as may be seen from the terms of the judgment therein, an extract from which is quoted ante, p. 48) dealt with the duty of preventing the escape from one's land of something likely to do harm. In the other, the wider, class of cases, responsibility is not confined to the escape of objects likely to do harm but extends to the mere keeping of such an object. This May v. Burdett clearly shows. "It was said, indeed, further, on the part of the defendant, that the monkey being an animal ferae naturae he would not be answerable for injuries committed by it, if it escaped and went at large without any default on the part of the defendant during the time it had so escaped and was at large, because at that time it would not be in his keeping nor under his control; but we cannot allow any weight to this objection; for in the first place, there is no statement in the declaration that the monkey had escaped, and it is expressly averred that the injury occurred whilst the defendant kept it; we are, besides, of opinion, as already stated, that the defendant, if he would keep it was bound to keep it secure at all events[1]."

[1] The Court, in effect, refused to adopt and apply to the case of dangerous animals the rules which obtained in the Roman law with regard to the escape of animals ferae naturae. The truth is that in this connection the terms ferae naturae and domitae naturae are used in English law in a different sense to that of the Roman law. For the purposes of ownership, a monkey is an animal ferae naturae, and so is a rabbit for example, but different considerations apply in English law to the case of the escape of each.

Further, the absolute duty to prevent harm by dangerous animals is distinguished from the other cases of strict responsibility in two particulars: first, as a rule the wrong consists simply in the doing the act which results in harm; in the case of the keeping of animals a further element is necessary before the duty is violated, namely the element of knowledge. Secondly, in the general case where the law raises an absolute duty, the act of the person responsible in exposing others to the extraordinary risk is not of itself a wrongful act. In the special case of animals, the act of keeping the animal, without more, is (semble) a wrongful act.

The law has always insisted that liability for harm caused by animals (apart from trespass or negligence) should be based upon the existence of the fact of knowledge, on the part of the owner, of a propensity to cause harm of the kind which actually has occurred. This knowledge in one class of cases must be alleged and proved; in another class of cases it is presumed by the law itself. The presumption in the latter case, like the presumption of negligence referred to above, is a praesumptio juris et de jure, that is to say, one for whose rebuttal no evidence may be given. The grounds for liability thus contain a personal element— an element, moreover, which is anomalous in this respect, that it occurs in connection with civil responsibility. If the law had cast upon the person who keeps animals the duty of insurance simpliciter, without regard to knowledge of a propensity to do the kind of harm which has occurred, the principle of liability would have proceeded upon a more rational ground.

The second particular in which the case of injury by animals differs from the other cases of strict liability is the quality of the act which results in the injury. And this brings us to the origin of the rule of absolute liability in these animal cases. The origin is not to be found in the principle laid down in Rylands v. Fletcher, but in the view taken in the earlier law that the keeping of a dangerous animal is in itself a wrongful act. Mr Salmond and Sir Frederick Pollock are both of opinion that the view that the very act of keeping a dangerous animal is itself wrongful, and therefore a ground of liability if damage ensues, can no longer be accepted as sound. Mr Salmond at p. 388 of his work on Torts says: "Even in the case of wild beasts, there is nothing illegal in the possession of them. The keeping of a wild-beast show is a perfectly lawful business, no less than the keeping of cattle, yet tigers and cows will both do mischief after the custom of their kind if they are allowed the opportunity." But the law assumes that harmless animals like the cow do not do mischief at all, in the sense in which the matter is now being considered. If Mr Salmond's reasoning were correct there would be no point in the requirement of scienter, and the rules relating to that difficult branch of the law would be superfluous.

Sir Frederick Pollock instances the case of the Zoological Gardens which, in accordance with the present view, would be a public nuisance. As a matter of fact that instance was put by counsel for the defendant in May v. Burdett and it did not find sympathy with the Court.

If the keeping of a dangerous animal is not a wrong
in itself, it has been said that on principle no wrong
can come from it until some wrongful circumstance
intervenes: in other words, until there is negligence.
But it is undoubted law at the present day that allegation and proof of negligence are unnecessary. This
argument of course will not hold, for it might be said
that the intervening wrongful circumstance is not
negligence but the failure to prevent harm being caused.

What is the state of the authorities? There is
ample authority in the earlier cases for the proposition
that the keeping of an animal which is known to be
dangerous is in itself a wrongful act. For example:

(1) The form of the declaration in May v. Burdett
given on page 58 ante, and the extracts from the
judgment of Lord Denman quoted on the page following.

(2) The case of Jackson v. Smithson ([1846], 15 M.
& W. 563), where the declaration in case stated that "the
defendant wrongfully and injuriously kept a ram, well
knowing that he was prone and accustomed to attack,
butt and injure mankind; and that the said ram,
while the defendant so kept the same, attacked butted
and threw down and thereby hurt the plaintiff," this
was held sufficient on motion in arrest of judgment,
without any allegation or proof that the defendant
negligently kept the ram. The Court of Exchequer
Chamber held that they were bound by the decision of
May v. Burdett on this point. Counsel for defendant
clearly drew the attention of the court to the question
of the quality of the keeping. He pointed out that the
reasonable meaning of the mere allegation that the
defendant "wrongfully and injuriously" kept the

animal was, not that the defendant "improperly" kept the animal, but that it was an improper thing to keep it at all. In the course of his judgment, Mr Baron Platt said: "No doubt a man has a right to keep an animal which is ferae naturae, and no one has a right to interfere with him in doing so, until some mischief happens; but as soon as it has done an injury, then the keeping it becomes, as regards that person, an act for which he is responsible." This passage is often quoted as an authority for the view that the keeping a dangerous animal is not a wrongful act. But, in the first place, suppose the words to bear their literal meaning, then, even when so interpreted, it is submitted that the passage on examination will be found in no way inconsistent with the view of the other judges. The fact that the act is wrongful in itself does not make it wrongful with regard to any particular individual until he suffers harm as a consequence of it. The truth is, that the right of that individual against the owner of the animal is only a "qualified right," that is to say, a right to claim that the act shall not be done to his prejudice. Damage is an essential part of the action. But it may be objected that that would be an instance of "injuria sine damno," a position which cannot exist in law. The answer is that "injuria" in that phrase means not simply a breach of law, but that limited kind of breach of law which consists in the violation of another's private rights. It is submitted that when the learned judge made the remarks concerning animals ferae naturae he could not have had sufficiently in mind the case of animals which are dangerous by nature and are universally recognised to be so.   Otherwise he would have been enunciating a proposition directly opposed to the law of May v. Burdett by the decision in which case the Court of which he was a member expressed itself to be bound.

(3) In Card v. Case ([1848], 5 C.B. 622), counsel said, arguendo, that the keeping a savage dog or other ferocious animal, per se, is not a wrongful act; the wrongful act is, the so keeping it as to cause injury: the gist of the action is the negligent keeping. Mr Justice Maule interposed with the following remarks: "You are directly at issue with May v. Burdett and Jackson v. Smithson.   The allegation of duty is quite immaterial.   (Brown v. Mallett [1848], 5 C.B. 599.) The utmost diligence will not excuse the defendant, if the dog was of a ferocious disposition and the defendant knew it....In the three last cited cases [Taverner v. Little (5 N.C. 678), Dunford v. Trattles ([1844], 12 M. & W. 529) and Hart v. Crowley ([1840], 12 A. & E. 378)] apart from the injury, the proprietorship of the cart, the ship, and the waggon was innocent. If you can convince us that the keeping a ferocious dog is an innocent thing, you will have made some way." Counsel then put the case of a person keeping poison, or a loaded gun, and mischief resulting.   And per Maule J.: "There the act would not be unlawful, unless there were culpable negligence."

In delivering judgment Coltman J. said: "What is the wrongful act here alleged?   Looking at the frame of this declaration, it may be said that the negligently keeping the dog was the wrongful act charged; but that is overlooking that which is the

gist and substance of the action. It is clear from the
case of May v. Burdett—where the matter underwent
very great consideration—that the circumstance of
the defendant's keeping the animal negligently, is not
essential; but that the gravamen is, the keeping a
ferocious animal, knowing its propensities, and the
consequent injury to the plaintiff....In the present
case the wrongful act was not the negligent mode of
keeping the dog, but the keeping it at all knowing its
ferocious disposition." Mr Justice Maule was of the
same opinion. "Now the cases of May v. Burdett and
Jackson v. Smithson, and the general course of precedents and authorities referred to in the former case,
prove that the wrongful act is, the keeping a ferocious
dog, knowing its savage disposition, and that an
action of this sort may be maintained without alleging
any negligence. The declaration here, idly and super-
fluously, states a duty to arise on the defendant's
part—as in Brown v. Mallett ([1848], 5 C.B. 599)—to
use due and reasonable care and precaution in and
about the keeping and management of the dog....It
may be that the allegation of negligence, coupled with
the consequent damage to the plaintiff, would show a
cause of action. Here, however, there is no doubt
that the declaration contains a sufficient allegation of a
cause of action. It states a wrongful act—the keeping
a ferocious dog, knowing its disposition—and damage
to the plaintiff."

(4) In the recent case of Baker v. Snell, Sutton J.
in the Divisional Court ([1908] 2 K.B. 352) and Cozens-
Hardy M.R. and Farwell L.J. in the Court of Appeal
([1908] 2 K.B. 825) were all of opinion that it is a

wrongful act to keep an animal which is known to be dangerous, and their judgments in that case were founded on that opinion.

On the other hand, besides the dicta of Platt B. in Card v. Case which have been already dealt with, there is some authority against the view that the keeping a dangerous animal is a wrongful act.

In the old cases of Brock v. Copeland ([1794], 1 Esp. 203) and Sarch v. Blackburn ([1830], 4 Car. & P. 297), Lord Kenyon and Tindal C.J. respectively were of opinion that a person has a right to keep a fierce and dangerous dog for the protection of his property. In Baker v. Snell (supra), Kennedy L.J. adopted the dicta of Platt B. in Card v. Case, and held that there is nothing culpable or wrong in keeping an animal ferae naturae, that is, a dangerous animal. But he also stated that the gist of the action was the scienter, and this is directly in the face of dicta in the cases of May v. Burdett, Jackson v. Smithson and Card v. Case that the gist of the action is the keeping the animal after knowledge.

In the still more recent case of Clinton v. Lyons ([1912] 3 K.B. 198), Bray J. remarked that the dictum of Farwell L.J. in Baker v. Snell went too far in his opinion, and he refused to hold that it is a wrongful act to keep a cat which, whilst with kittens, is dangerous to dogs. With respect, it may be said that his reasons for so holding are not quite to the point.

In the result, having regard to the clearly expressed opinions in the earlier cases, that the same have never been overruled or even directly doubted until quite recently, and that there is an opinion of the Court of

Appeal in favour of the view, it is submitted that the law is still that the keeping of a dangerous animal is a wrongful act, whatever may be the consequences of such a rule.

The matter is important when we come to consider what exceptions there are to liability.

2. (1) The person who keeps a domestic or harmless animal is not liable (apart from negligence or trespass) for harm caused by acts which the animal has a natural tendency to commit.

(2) Moreover, at common law, no liability (apart from negligence or trespass) attaches to him for harm caused by acts of a vicious or mischievous character which are foreign to the ordinary nature of such an animal. But if he knows that the particular animal possesses a propensity or disposition to commit acts of that character, either generally or under special circumstances, then he keeps the animal at his peril and becomes absolutely liable for any harm which may ensue. Proof of such knowledge is technically called "proof of the scienter."

(3) Apart from statute, liability does not depend upon ownership but upon possession. He who keeps or controls the animal is responsible, and the question whether he keeps or controls the animal is one of fact. It is a

sufficient "keeping" if he harbour the animal or habitually allow it to have access to his premises. But no liability accrues to the occupier for the acts of an animal which strays upon his premises, if nothing has been done to encourage its presence or reasonable care has been taken to prevent its continued access.

The rules as to the determination of liability for acts of harm by domestic animals or animals harmless by nature are more complex than those relating to dangerous animals, and involve fine distinctions, particularly in regard to proof of knowledge. Broadly it may be stated that, apart from liability in trespass or for negligence, the person who keeps such an animal is not liable (1) for acts which are ordinarily committed by such animals, or (2) for acts which are not usually committed by such animals because they are not within the ordinary nature of that species of animals. But he becomes responsible for acts of the latter character which cause injury or damage, upon proof that at the time of the commission of the act, he knew that the particular animal possessed a propensity or disposition to commit acts of that character.

It is usual and convenient to speak of the "owner" of the animal as being the person liable, for in the majority of cases the animal is in his possession or under his control. But as is stated above, liability does not depend upon ownership; and this fact should be borne in mind in reading these pages where the term "owner" is constantly being used.

The liability for trespass of animals has already been adverted to, and the question for what consequences of such trespass the liability extends has been considered. Cases have been dealt with and numerous authorities have been quoted to show that a person is liable for the direct consequences of such trespass but not for remote consequences. A person is liable for the damage done by his cattle or other animals trespassing on another's close and doing damage of the kind which might be expected of them, such as trampling down crops or eating herbage. Such damage is that which it is the ordinary nature of such animals to commit, is therefore not too remote, and may be recovered for in the action of trespass.

The same is the case if we turn to the law of negligence. A person is liable for the ordinary acts of his animals under circumstances which cast upon him the duty of taking care to prevent the committal of such acts. Therefore a person who negligently leaves his horse unattended in the street is responsible if it moves on and in so doing causes harm, as for instance by a collision. (Illidge v. Goodwin [1831], 5 C. & P. 190; Whatman v. Pearson [1868], L.R. 3 C.P. 422.)

But apart from trespass or negligence, the owner of the animal is not responsible for damage caused by acts which it is natural to a domestic or ordinarily harmless animal to commit. To put the matter briefly, there is no liability in such a case under what may be called "the rule in May v. Burdett." A different view appears to be taken by Mr Salmond on this point. In his treatise on the law of Torts (third edition, p. 383 et seq.) he states that all harm done by

animals is of two kinds: (1) harm which is natural to
that species of animal; (2) harm which is not natural
to the species, but which is nevertheless done by the
particular animal in question. "In the first case the
owner of the animal is not permitted to allege that
he did not know of its tendency to do the mischief;
he is conclusively presumed to have known the ordinary
character of that species of animal; nor is it any
defence to him that he had good reason to believe that
the individual animal had no tendency to do such
harm, although natural to the species. In the second
case, on the other hand, actual knowledge of the
tendency of the individual animal to do the harm
which it did must be proved by the plaintiff....Thus
it is a natural tendency of cattle to stray and trespass,
and eat and tread down crops; and it is the natural
tendency of tigers and other wild beasts to attack
mankind and other animals. In such a case, therefore,
no proof of scienter is necessary. Knowledge is
presumed by the law, and this presumption is conclusive
so as even to exclude evidence that the individual
animal was reasonably believed to have no tendency
to act after the manner of its kind. On the other hand,
it is not the natural tendency of dogs to bite human
beings; therefore it is necessary for the plaintiff in
such a case to prove that the defendant actually knew
that the dog was dangerous and had departed from
the peaceable habit of its species." On page 386 of
the same work he further says: "Provided that there
exists the necessary knowledge of danger, in accordance
with the rule which we have considered in the preceding
section, he who keeps an animal is absolutely responsible

for its acts. He is bound at his peril to prevent it from going at large or in any other manner having an opportunity of exercising its mischievous instincts. If any harm is done by it, he is liable (unless there exists some specific ground of exemption) without any allegation or proof of negligence in the custody or care of the animal. This rule of absolute liability was established in the year 1846 by the Court of Queen's Bench in May v. Burdett...."

With respect it is submitted that Mr Salmond has approached the question of the common law or absolute liability (scil. the so-called rule in May v. Burdett) from the wrong standpoint. The view here taken is that liability depends on the knowledge of the quality of the animal rather than the quality of the act committed by it. The question whether a particular act is a vicious or mischievous act[1] in the case of an ordinarily harmless animal is, of course, pertinent, as such an act is the occasion of liability; but the cause or ground of liability is the known dangerous quality or propensity of the animal.

The so-called rule in May v. Burdett has nothing whatsoever to do with liability for acts natural to a domestic or harmless animal. If there be any responsibility for such acts it can only be because they are the direct consequences of trespass or negligence.

In the case of Clinton v. J. Lyons & Company ([1912] 3 K.B. 198) the plaintiff, who was carrying a pet dog, entered, by permission of defendants, one of their tea-shops. On the premises was a cat which

---

[1] Surely he uses these terms in a different sense from that in which they are ordinarily employed.

had kittens.   The cat had been shut up in a store-room but got out, and when plaintiff put her dog on the floor the cat sprang on the dog and bit it.   The plaintiff picked up the dog and handed it to her husband who was with her.   The cat then sprang on her shoulder and bit her arm.   In an action for damages for the injuries to the plaintiff and to her dog, it was held, as far as the injuries to the dog were concerned, that the act of the cat was one natural to its species, and that therefore the defendants were not liable.

In the course of his judgment, with which on this point Ridley J. expressly agreed, Bray J. said: "It remains to consider whether there was any evidence to support the claim for damages for injuries to her dog.   Now it is certainly the common experience of mankind that cat and dog will fight whether the cat has kittens or not, but it would be ridiculous to hold that for that reason every person who keeps a dog or a cat does so at his peril and is responsible for any damage his cat will do to his neighbour's dog or his dog will do to his neighbour's cat.   There is no case to be found in the books showing such a liability." ([1912], 81 L.J. (K.B.) at p. 931[1].)

The instance which Mr Salmond gives of the ordinary acts of a person's domestic animals for which he holds that their owner is responsible under the

---

[1] Supposing the cat (or a dog) had even been a trespasser, and, whilst trespassing, had committed such an injury as that in the case just cited, presumably its owner would not have been responsible. But this would have been owing to the special rule affecting the trespass of dogs (and possibly cats) which was noticed ante, pp. 33–36, and certainly would not affect the general rule which is con tended for here.

so-called rule in May v. Burdett—namely, the natural
tendency of cattle to stray and trespass, and eat and
tread down crops—is an indication that he takes a
different view from that expressed here as to what is
now the true ground of the common law liability.
At pp. 388–389 he considers the origin of the absolute
liability for cattle-trespass—which is said to have
given rise to the rule in Rylands v. Fletcher; and the
origin of the absolute liability for injury by animals—
which gave rise to the rule in May v. Burdett; and he
shows that they proceeded from entirely unconnected
principles, being independent growths from different
roots. And yet he gives as an illustration of the
latter an instance which is not covered by it, but
obviously belongs to the former. He also examines
the logical relation which exists between the two rules
at the present day, and concludes that they largely
overlap each other, if they do not actually coincide.
"It seems probable," he says, "that there is no case
in which a person can be liable under Rylands v.
Fletcher, for damage done by an animal in which he
will not be equally liable under the more comprehensive
rule in May v. Burdett." It is submitted, however,
that this view cannot be maintained. For the reasons
already mentioned it seems that all cases of harm
resulting from acts which it is within the ordinary
nature of a domestic or harmless animal to commit
are instances where the owner of such an animal would
be liable under Rylands v. Fletcher, but not under the
rule in May v. Burdett. If such harm were the ordinary
consequence of trespass or negligence it would be
remediable in an action for damages; otherwise not.

The rule in May v. Burdett cannot therefore be said
to be more comprehensive than the rule in Rylands v.
Fletcher.

Extracts have already been quoted from the
judgment of Lord Esher M.R. in Filburn's case which
show that the law assumes that certain animals are
not of a ferocious or dangerous disposition. These
may be divided into two groups, viz. (*a*) those which
are harmless by nature, e.g. rabbits, hares, partridges,
pheasants and the like; (*b*) those which are recognised
by the law as not being dangerous in England. They
are rendered harmless by being domesticated for
generations, e.g. horses and cattle. To make the
owner liable for acts committed by such animals, if the
acts are of a vicious or mischievous kind, knowledge
of the propensity of the animal must be strictly proved.
This rule has come down to us from the very earliest
cases and has maintained its integrity in the common
law in spite of criticism from without and deprecation
from within. It has required the force of the Legis-
lature to interfere with it, and even then the interference is partial and by way of exception merely, the
result being that an added prominence is given to the
general rule.

1 Dyer 2 *b*, pl. 162. "The master of a dog which
has killed sheep is not punishable unless he knew it to
be mischievous. Note, that in evidence to an inquest
it was agreed by Fitzherbert and Shelley, That if a
man have a dog which has killed sheep, the master of
the dog being ignorant of the quality and property of
the dog, the master shall not be punished for that
killing; otherwise is it if he have notice of the quality

of the dog." In this case one "William Morgan, Knight, impleaded John Cronet for chasing his pigs and sheep with dogs at Sambro', and for the biting of the said dogs, so that the said sheep died; the jurors said that the aforesaid John was not guilty, nor did command his servants, nor was it done by his command but as for the biting of one of the sheep, of the price of five shillings and eightpence, his servants did this; and the jurors, being demanded whether the aforesaid dogs were accustomed thus to bite without any instigation, said positively that they were not; wherefore let the plaintiff take nothing by his writ, and let John go thereof without day."

So in Buxendin v. Sharp (2 Salk. 662)[1] "the plaintiff declared that the defendant kept a bull which used to run at men; but did not say sciens or scienter etc. This was held naught after a verdict; for the action lies not unless the master knows of this quality, and we cannot intend it was proved at the trial, for the plaintiff need not prove more than is in his declaration." A case of Bayntine v. Sharp (1 Lutw. 33) seems to be almost identical with the foregoing. "Case, against the defendant for keeping a mad bull, which wounded the plaintiff. He had a verdict but the judgment was arrested because it was not alleged that the defendant did know the bull to be mad." The following note is added: "It doth not appear when this case was adjudged nor in what Court, neither is there any Book cited in it." In the case of Mason v. Keeling ([1700], 1 Ld Raym. 606) the declaration stated that defendant "Quendam canem

---

[1] See also Buxentine v. Sharp (3 Salk. 12).

molossum, Anglice a mongril mastiff, valde ferocem
custodivit et retinuit et canem illum in communi
platea vocata Water Street ore ejusdem canis adtunc
minime ligato existente, Anglice not musled, libere et
ad largum ire permisit idem canis pro defectu debitae
curae et custodiae ipsius the defendant ipsum the
plaintiff per communem plateam apud etc circa legitima
negotia sua transeuntem furiose et violenter impetivit,
et ipsum the plaintiff adtunc et ibidem graviter momordit et vulneravit, et suram, Anglice the calf, cruris
sinistri ipsius the plaintiff graviter momordit et vulneravit, etc." Defendant's counsel took exception to
the declaration "that the plaintiff has not shown that
the defendant knew that this dog was valde ferox;
without which knowledge he shall not be answerable
for any injury, that he of a sudden and unknown to
the defendant, did to the plaintiff." For plaintiff it
was urged "that though in such actions as this here,
it has been held necessary in many cases to say sciens
in the declaration; yet where the fact has such circumstances as this hath, the omitting of sciens will not
vitiate the declaration. For in this case the dog is
shown to be valde ferox; and then to permit such a
dog to go at large in the highway is a common nuisance;
and then whosoever receives any particular prejudice
or damage shall have an action." And per Holt C.J.
and Turton J. "the declaration is ill for want of showing
that the defendant had notice, that the dog was fierce.
...Now for anything that appears to the contrary,
the owner might not have had this dog but one day or
two before and did not know of this fierce nature; and
then the dog, because the door was left open, ran out

and bit the plaintiff; it will be very hard to subject
this defendant the owner to an action for it.   Otherwise
if the defendant had known before that this dog was
of such a fierce nature, for he ought to have kept him
in at his peril....But Gould J. was of opinion that
the declaration was good; because the averring, that
the dog was fierce, made the owner liable to an action
for an injury done by such dog, because he did not
keep him in a safe place." Sed adjournatur. And
afterwards the parties agreed between themselves and
no judgment was given[1].

The case is important upon another ground, to
which notice has already been drawn in a previous
section, Holt C.J. having given utterance to certain
propositions the meaning of which in this connection is
far from clear.   He is reported to have said: "There
is a great difference between horses and oxen, in which
a man has a valuable property and which are not so
familiar to mankind, and dogs; the former the owner
ought to confine, and take all reasonable caution, that
they do no mischief, otherwise an action will lie
against him; but otherwise of dogs, before he has notice
of some mischievous quality."

Willes J. in Cox v. Burbidge ([1863], 13 C.B. (N.S.)
430) thought that the expression "a valuable property"
had reference to the passage to be found in the Insti-
tutes IV. Tit. 9, "Denique si ursus fugit a domino et
sic nocuit, non potest quondam dominus conveniri,
quia desinit dominus esse, ubi fera evasit," and he gives
reasons why that could not apply to dogs.   Willes J.

---

[1] In 12 Mod. 336, the Court is represented to have given judgment for the defendant.

thought that perhaps control was meant by Lord Holt and not property. However that may be, "the dictum exhausts itself on the liability of the owners of horses and oxen for trespasses committed by them on land, pursuing their ordinary instincts in search of food." The dictum cannot affect the liability for injuries by domestic or harmless animals, for Lord Holt goes on to put the very case of a horse as one where the owner is not liable unless he knows of the vice. "But in the former case if the owner puts a horse or an ox to grass in his field, which is adjoining to the highway and the horse or the ox breaks the hedge, and runs into the highway and kicks or gores some passenger, an action will not lie against the owner: otherwise if he had notice, that they had done such a thing before."

For a clear contrast between the rules of liability in the case of a dangerous animal and in the case of a harmless animal the reader is again referred to the extracts from the case of R. v. Huggins (ante, p. 57).

Presumably the earliest instance where the distinction was taken between acts which are, and acts which are not, within the ordinary nature of the animal, occurs in the case of Jenkins v. Turner ([1696], 2 Salk. 662). "The plaintiff declared that the defendant kept a boar ad mordend. animalia consuet., and knew of this habit and that the boar did bite etc. This was held good after verdict, though it was objected that these animals may be frogs or mice etc. for we must intend there was proof of biting such animals as will support the action, otherwise the judge and jury would not have concurred in this verdict whereby the plaintiff recovers damages; And as to another

objection, viz. that the defendant cannot know what
animals he is to defend against; it was answered, that
no evidence can be given of killing any animals but
what he has knowledge of."

In another report of the same case, Powell J. is
represented to have said: "There may be a difference
between a boar and a dog; for it is the nature of a
dog to kill animals which are ferae naturae as hares,
cats etc.; but it is not natural to a boar to kill anything; and therefore in the case of a dog there might
have been a question whether the word animalia had
been good in the declaration, because it might have
been intended of some such animals as they naturally
bite and kill. But since a boar does not naturally
kill any it shall be intended as before is said."
(1 Ld Raym. 110.) Though this case was not cited by
counsel in Clinton v. Lyons (ante, p. 70), yet the Court
there adopted a similar view, namely that it is not a
vicious or mischievous act for a dog to injure a cat, or
vice versa. Such an act is one within the ordinary
nature of such an animal to commit, and, apart from
trespass or negligence, involves no liability.

In an action upon the case, reported in Cro. Car. 254,
for keeping a mastiff "sciens that he was 'assuetus ad
mordendum porcos' and that the plaintiff was possessed
of a sow great with pigs and that the said mastiff bit
the said sow so as she died of the biting," it was moved
in arrest of judgment that the declaration was bad "for
it is proper for a dog to hunt hogs out of the ground;
and his biting of the hogs is necessary, and not like to
the keeping of a dog which usually bites sheep or other
cattle. But the Court, absente Richardson, conceived

the action well lies; for it is not lawful to keep dogs to bite and kill swine. Wherefore it was adjudged for the plaintiff."

The following cases are illustrative of what, in modern law, are considered to be mischievous or vicious acts, that is to say, acts of harm which it is not within the ordinary nature of the particular animal to commit. To make the owner of the animal liable for the harm received the scienter must be proved by evidence the degree and sufficiency of which will be indicated in subsequent pages.

In an action for injury caused by a vicious bull, it appeared that the plaintiff, with a boy, was driving a cow "in a particular state" past a field in which the bull was kept when the bull crossed the intervening ditch and approached the cow. Plaintiff struck the bull which threw him down and injured him. Notice had been given to defendant of the bull's having run at a man previously and the scienter was otherwise sufficently proved. Chief Justice Best, in his summing up, said to the jury: "If you are satisfied upon the whole, that the injury occurred from the vicious nature of the bull, which the defendant knew, then you will find your verdict for the plaintiff." (Blackman v. Simmons [1827], 3 Car. & P. 138.)

Similarly, it is a vicious act on the part of a ram to butt a person, and the scienter is therefore an essential to liability. (Jackson v. Smithson [1846], 15 M. & W. 563.) But after proof of scienter the animal is in the same category with regard to injuries as is an animal dangerous by nature. Mr Baron Alderson recognised this in this very case. "In truth there is no distinction between the case of an animal which breaks through the tameness of its nature and is fierce, and known by the owner to be so, and one which is ferae naturae."

It is not the ordinary habit of a horse to kick a child on a highway. This is "a sudden act of a fierce and violent nature which is altogether contrary to the usual habits of the horse," and the owner is not responsible for such an act in the absence of proof of scienter. (Cox v. Burbidge [1863], 32 L.J. (C.P.) 89.)

The scienter is also an essential in an action for damages for the destruction of game by dogs. (Read v. Edwards [1864], 17 C.B. (N.S.) 245.) The law with regard to the destruction or injury of cattle by dogs has been modified by statute and will be considered in detail at a later place.

An animal which infects other animals with disease is in the same position as an animal which does any other kind of injury, and therefore knowledge of its character for harm is to be proved in order to establish liability. In an action for "wrongfully, negligently and improperly" keeping sheep diseased with the scab and dangerous to be at large, defendant "well knowing that the said sheep were so diseased," etc., whereby the sheep became intermixed with plaintiff's healthy sheep and infected them with disease, proof of scienter is essential to the support of the action. (Cooke v. Waring [1863], 9 T.L.R. 257.) The Court also held in this case that there can be no negligence in a matter of this sort if there was no knowledge on defendant's part, at the time of the supposed negligence in keeping them, that the sheep were then diseased;

and in the absence of evidence of such knowledge that
a nonsuit was rightly directed. (See also Earp v.
Faulkner [1875], 34 L.T. (N.S.) 284.)

It is to be noted that the requirement of scienter
exists in the law of tort only. A person who enters
into a contract to take due care in respect of the person
or property of another is liable, in case he has omitted
to take such care, for damage caused by the acts of
dangerous animals, and this independently of any
proof of scienter. Thus in Smith v. Cook ([1875],
1 Q.B.D. 79) the defendant, an agister of cattle, had
received a horse from the plaintiff to be taken care of
for reward. He placed the plaintiff's horse in a field
with a number of heifers, knowing that a bull, kept on
adjoining land, had several times been found in the
field, the shallow ditch between the two closes not
being sufficient to keep it out. There was no evidence
that the bull was of a mischievous disposition. The
horse was found dead, apparently having been gored
by the bull. In an action against the defendant for
breach of contract to take reasonable care, the jury
found for the plaintiff. A rule nisi having been
obtained on the ground that there was no evidence of
scienter and that such evidence was necessary to
maintain the action, the rule was discharged by the
Court on the ground that knowledge of the mischievous
disposition of the bull was not essential to liability
under the contract of agistment. Blackburn J. said:
"The question is: Does this principle (i.e. the principle
requiring proof of scienter) oblige us to hold as a
matter of law that it cannot be negligence on the part
of an agister of horses to assume that bulls and cows

are likely to be quiet, and to put a horse among them? I think that this proposition is a non sequitur upon the law as to mischievous animals. I do not say that the defendant's act would in all cases necessarily be negligence, but it is a question of fact whether he took sufficient care or not, and the doctrine of scienter which, I have said, depends mainly upon authority, ought not to be extended to a contract to take reasonable care."

In the treatment of the principles set forth at the head of this part of this work liability for injury by harmless animals has been said to attach to the person who "keeps" the animal, i.e. has possession or control of it. This person may or may not be the owner.

In an old case it was established that any person who harbours the animal or habitually allows it to have access to his premises may be liable as for "keeping" it. "It is not material whether the defendant was the owner of the dog or not; if he kept it, that is sufficient; and the harbouring a dog about one's premises or allowing him to be or resort there, is a sufficient keeping of the dog to support this form of action. It was the defendant's duty either to have destroyed the dog or to have sent him away, as soon as he found that he was mischievous." (McKone v. Wood [1831], 5 Car. & P. 1.)[1] It is to be noted that in the foregoing case the defendant *alone* had control of the dog, to the exclusion of the owner, and his liability has been explained on that ground. Presumably the owner

[1] Lord Tenterden C.J., from whose judgment this extract is quoted, apparently had no doubt that the keeping a dog in such circumstances was a wrongful act.

would not have been held liable if the action had been brought against him.

In the recent case of North v. Wood ([1914], 83 L.J. (K.B.) 587) defendant's daughter, who was seventeen years old and lived with her father assisting him in his business and receiving a weekly wage for so doing, owned a bull terrier which was kept at defendant's house. The dog licence was in the daughter's name, and she paid for it and for the dog's food out of her own money. Whilst the plaintiff was leading her Pomeranian dog past defendant's shop the bull terrier attacked and killed the other dog. Both the defendant and his daughter knew that the bull terrier had previously bitten two Pomeranian dogs. In an action for damages it was held that defendant's daughter had arrived at years of discretion and was able to control the bull terrier and that in fact she had the control of it, and that therefore the defendant who was not the owner was not liable. On appeal the decision was affirmed by the Divisional Court, the opinion being expressed at the same time that if the daughter had not been competent to control the animal the defendant would have been the person liable.

The question as to who "keeps" or has the control of the animal is therefore one of fact. But in a case of ambiguous control it seems as if "control follows ownership."

But if the animal has strayed on to one's premises and there causes injury, no liability ensues if nothing has been done to encourage its presence, or at any rate if reasonable care has been used to prevent its continued access to the premises. The question resolves itself into whether the person sought to be made responsible has taken reasonable care to render his premises safe for those persons who may lawfully resort to them. (Smith v. Great Eastern Railway Co. [1866], L.R. 2 C.P. 4.) In this case the plaintiff had been bitten by a stray dog whilst at defendants' railway station waiting for a train. It was proved that at 9 p.m. the same evening the dog had attacked another person on the platform and had torn her dress and that the attention of the Railway Company's employees had been called to the matter; that an hour and a half later the dog had attacked a cat in the signal-box, near the station, and the porter had then kicked the dog out and that nothing more was seen of it until it attacked the plaintiff at 11.30 p.m. On these facts it was held that there was no evidence to warrant a jury in finding that the Railway Company had been guilty of negligence. "It is not enough to show that the damage may have occurred through the negligence of the defendants' servants—even coupled with the suggestion that no sufficient explanation was given of the dog's conduct. The plaintiff must show something which the defendants might have done, and which they omitted to do, before they can be held responsible for the misfortune which has happened to her." (Willes J. at p. 10.)

3.   (1) In proving the scienter it is essential to establish knowledge of a propensity or disposition of the particular animal to commit an act of the kind which effects the injury or causes the damage complained of.

(2) Evidence of scienter must tend to establish knowledge of the particular propensity or disposition to which the vicious or mischievous act is referable. Thus in the case of a dog biting a human being it must be shown that the animal was "accustomed to bite mankind" and that the owner knew this.

It has already been stated that scienter is the owner's knowledge of a propensity or disposition of the animal to commit an act of the kind which effects the injury or causes the damage complained of. It is not a simple matter to gather any general principles from the consideration of the cases bearing on this point. At most it may be laid down that the evidence must tend to establish the particular propensity from which the vicious or mischievous act flows, e.g. a propensity to chase and kill game.

In the case of injury to human beings it is sufficient to show that the animal has once, to the owner's knowledge, previously committed a like injury. If a person keeps a dog after notice that it has once bitten a man, an action will lie against him at the suit of a person who is subsequently bitten by the dog. (Smith v. Pelah, 2 Str. 1264.) And so the Chief Justice here ruled "though it happened by such person's treading on the dog's toes, for it was owing to his not hanging the dog on the first notice. And the safety of the King's subjects ought not to be endangered[1]."

---

[1] Evidently he also was of opinion that the mere keeping of such a dog was a wrongful act.

More modern cases have shown that, even though it be proved that the animal has bitten a person previously to the owner's knowledge, it is, nevertheless, a question for the jury to decide whether the dog was a ferocious one or not, and if so, whether the defendant knew it. The propensity is not inferred from the previous bite as a matter of law. The circumstances of the case must be considered and evidence of provocation of the animal will be received. (Charlwood v. Grieg [1850], 3 Car. & K. 46.)

Is it necessary to go so far as this, however; is it necessary to show an actual injury such as a previous bite, or will evidence falling short of this suffice?

The Courts have held over and over again that knowledge of an actual injury need not be shown. Then the question arises, What facts must be shown to have been within the owner's knowledge? This can be answered only by considering the circumstances of each case. The quantum of evidence necessary to show that the animal is possessed of a ferocious or mischievous disposition has differed at the different stages of the law's development, and with a fine disregard of principle.

The two matters are so closely allied that it seems almost impossible to consider what is evidence of knowledge apart from what evidence is necessary to establish the propensity. In Mason v. Keeling (ante, p. 33) the majority of the Court held that it was insufficient to aver simply that the dog was "valde ferox."

Knowledge of something is essential. The question appears to be whether the animal had a previous mischievous or vicious propensity directed to the kind of harm inflicted, and whether the defendant knew of it. It is a question for the Court to decide whether there is evidence in law to go to the jury, and it is for the jury to decide upon the facts presented. In an action on the case the declaration of which charged the defendant with knowingly keeping a fierce and savage dog without being properly secured, by which the plaintiff's child was bit and torn and in consequence thereof died per quod servitium amisit, Lord Kenyon C.J. allowed evidence to go to the jury of a common report that defendant's dog had previously been bitten by a mad dog. The defendant's dog had been tied up in a cellar belonging to him, but the rope or chain by which it was fastened was of such a length that it permitted the dog to go as far as the curb-stone on the opposite side of the street. The dog broke through a little wicker gate into the street and injured the plaintiff's child. It was carried to the salt water, but after its return was seized with hydrophobia and died. His lordship said: "Such a case as this I believe never appeared before, but I am clearly of opinion the action is maintainable. Report had said the dog had been bitten by a mad dog; it became the duty of the defendant to be very circumspect; whether the dog was mad or not was matter of suspicion; but it is not sufficient to say, 'I did use a certain precaution.' He ought to use such as would put it out of the animal's power to do hurt; here too the defendant showed a knowledge that the animal was fierce, unruly, and not safe to be permitted to go abroad, by the precaution he used to tie him up; that precaution has not been sufficient; and for want of it the injury complained of has happened. I am clearly of opinion the plaintiff is entitled to recover." (Jones v. Perry [1796], 2 Esp. 482.)

In contrast with the foregoing is the case of Beck v. Dyson ([1815], 4 Camp. 198) nineteen years later. Case, for keeping a dog which bit the plaintiff. It was proved that the dog was of a fierce and savage disposition, that the defendant generally kept it tied up, and that the plaintiff, having been bitten by the dog, was promised a pecuniary recompense by the defendant; but there was no proof of the dog's having bitten any person previously. Lord Ellenborough held the evidence insufficient to warrant the jury in inferring that the dog was accustomed to bite within the knowledge of defendant, and directed a nonsuit.

In Judge v. Cox ([1816], 1 Starkie 285) the declaration in case averred the keeping a dog which the defendant knew to be accustomed to bite mankind and which severely bit the plaintiff's leg. It was proved that defendant was well aware of the dog's savage disposition, and in consequence had warned one of the witnesses to take care of the dog lest he should be bitten. Evidence was also given that subsequently to the injury complained of, the dog had bitten a child, but we are not told in the report whether this fact was put to the jury. Upon general principles such evidence ought not to have been admitted. Abbott J. after commenting on the fact that the defendant had expressed a warning to the witness to take care of the dog, left it to the jury to say whether they were satisfied that the dog had, before the time of the

injury, bitten some human being, and that the
defendant knew it. A verdict was given for the
plaintiff.

Hartley v. Harriman ([1818], 1 B. & Ald. 620) comes
next in point of date and the case is a more complicated
one owing to defective pleading. The Court of Queen's
Bench (Lord Ellenborough C.J., Bayley, Abbott and
Holroyd J.J.) there decided that evidence of dogs
being of a ferocious and mischievous disposition and
accustomed to attack men did not support an averment
that they were accustomed to "hunt, chase, bite,
worry and kill sheep and lambs." Evidence was given
that the dogs had previously attacked men, and in
one instance, that a voice had been heard from defendant's premises calling them off, and that they had on
previous occasions run after sheep. But there was no
proof that they had ever bitten or worried any sheep
before the event which gave rise to the action. Lord
Ellenborough ruled that the plaintiff had put himself
out of court by the allegation in the declaration of the
particular habits of the dogs and of the defendant's
knowledge of those habits; and he went on to say:
"He might perhaps have stated his ground of action
more generally by alleging that these dogs were of a
ferocious nature and unsafe to be left at large; and
there is evidence sufficient to show that the knowledge
which the defendant had of these dogs ought to have
imposed on him the duty of tying them up." Bayley J.
said: "The declaration might have been framed more
generally, and might have stated that these were dogs
of a ferocious and mischievous disposition, and then
there might have been evidence to support it. But

here it is stated that they were accustomed to bite
sheep and lambs. And there is no evidence of that
fact." The rule for a new trial was made absolute.
Apart from the decision in this particular instance, it
is difficult to see why a declaration in a case of injury
to animals should have been sufficient when framed
generally, whilst in the case of injury to mankind it
should have required to be framed specially. But in
any event this case does not affect the general principle
which is contended for here, namely, that the evidence
must be directed towards the particular mischievous
propensity which is the cause of the harm received.
As far as the form of the declaration is concerned, the
dictum of Powell J. in Jenkins v. Turner (ante, p. 82)
might be cited "that if a man has a dog which bites
sheep, and the man has notice of it and keeps the dog,
and afterwards it bites a mare, an action lies, but the
declaration must be special."

The case of Hartley v. Harriman was considered
in Gething v. Morgan (*The Law Times*, Vol. 29,
p. 106, [1857]), another case of sheep-worrying. It
was there proved that four years before the occurrence of the injury complained of, the same dogs
had, to defendant's knowledge, bitten a child eight
years old, who was passing through defendant's fold
in the daytime. The Court of Queen's Bench affirmed
a judgment for the plaintiff, Lord Campbell C.J.
adopting the dictum of Bayley J. that it would be
enough to allege that the dogs were of a ferocious
disposition to the knowledge of the owner, and
holding that there was sufficient evidence to support
that allegation. And per Crompton J.: "I agree that

the question is whether there was such evidence that a jury could fairly act upon, in finding for the plaintiff; and I think there was. In ordinary cases one previous act of ferocity is enough to put the owner on his guard; and if he afterwards permits his dogs, with knowledge of their vicious disposition, to run about, with tickets of leave as it were, he must be responsible for any further damage which they may do."

Although in English law an attack upon human beings can be given in evidence where it is necessary to prove a vicious disposition giving rise to an attack upon animals, and a propensity to attack animals of one species may be proved in support of an allegation of an attack on animals of another species, yet evidence of attacking or biting an animal is not evidence of a disposition to attack and bite mankind. (Osborne v. Chocqueel [1896], 2 Q.B. 109.) Here a dog had previously bitten a goat, to the knowledge of the defendant, and Lord Russell of Killowen C.J. and Wills J. held that in order to establish a cause of action it must be shown that defendant knew that the dog had a ferocious propensity directed against mankind. A finding that the dog was ferocious, based upon the fact of the attack on the goat, is insufficient. From the remarks of the judges on the argument of this case it is evident that they agreed with the principle contained in the rules set forth at the head of this section.

In Thomas v. Morgan ([1835], 2 C.M. & R. 496) the question was whether there was evidence to go to the jury of a scienter, where, on being informed that his dogs had bitten the plaintiff's cattle, defendant offered to settle for the damage done if it could be proved that his dogs had caused it. The question had previously arisen in almost similar terms in the case of Beck v. Dyson (ante, p. 93), where Lord Ellenborough refused to leave the evidence to the jury. It was proved in Thomas v. Morgan that the dogs had worried the cattle of other persons and were of a ferocious disposition. A witness also deposed that two or three days after the injury complained of the defendant's dogs had also worried his cattle, and that when complaint was made by witness, defendant said he could not help it, and that he had ordered his dogs to be kept up. This evidence was rejected by the Court on motion for leave to enter a verdict for the plaintiff who had been nonsuited. The Court held that proof that the dogs were of a savage disposition, and had bitten the cattle of other persons, was not evidence that the defendant *knew* that they were accustomed to bite cattle, but on the other hand that the evidence of the offer of compromise should have been left to the jury as some slight evidence of scienter, but should have been left to them with a strong observation in favour of the defendant. The rule was discharged on the ground that the evidence ought to have little or no weight with the jury, as the offer might have been made from motives of charity without any admission of liability at all.

Statements made by the owner of the animal at the time of or subsequently to the injury complained of have been held to be evidence to go to the jury of the scienter. (Cf. Judge v. Cox, ante, p. 93.)

In the case of Hudson v. Roberts ([1851], 6 Exch. 697) a person wearing a red handkerchief was walking in the public street and was attacked and injured by a bull which was being driven along with some cows belonging to the defendant. The defendant was proved to have said after the accident that the red handkerchief was the cause of it, for he knew that the bull would run at anything red. Another witness deposed that on a different occasion the defendant said he knew that *a* bull would run at anything red. Pollock C.B. delivered the judgment of the Court of Exchequer upon a motion to enter a nonsuit. The Court thought that either of the defendant's expressions was some evidence to go to the jury that he knew the animal was a dangerous one, and discharged the rule accordingly. The question arose in the case whether there was the same duty in regard to the keeping of the animal where the evidence went towards showing that the animal was ferocious only to a special class of mankind, namely, to those who are met with carrying a red handkerchief or wearing red garments. The Court, however, was not inclined to draw any such distinction between classes of persons: "As the circumstance of persons carrying red handkerchiefs is not uncommon, and it is reasonable to expect that in every public street persons so dressed may not unfrequently be met with, we think it was the duty of the defendant not to suffer such an animal to be driven in the public streets, possessing as he did the knowledge that, if it met a person with a red garment, it was likely to run at and injure him."

This case was relied upon in the recent case of Clinton v. Lyons (ante, p. 75), where it was contended that a cat must be accounted "ferae naturae" because it is vicious towards such of mankind as are carrying dogs. But Ridley J. said: "I think that a bull which is vicious to persons wearing a red tie may well attack a person without one. But the hostility of cat and dog, on the other hand, has passed into a proverb, and I am not disposed to say that if a cat attacks a dog, and by accident a person who happens to be there, the cat is therefore dangerous to mankind." ([1912], 81 L.J. (K.B.) at p. 926.)

The cases which turn upon the amount of evidence necessary to establish the vicious propensity and which are not concerned so much with the question of knowledge are numerous, and a few only of such cases may be cited here.

In an action for knowingly keeping a fierce and mischievous dog which had bitten or wounded the plaintiff, it is necessary to prove the injury to the plaintiff and that the dog was fierce and mischievous and known to be so by the plaintiff. A habit merely of bounding upon persons in play and seizing them, not so as to cause hurt or injury, though causing some annoyance and trivial accidental damage to clothes, is insufficient to sustain the action. (Line v. Taylor [1862], 3 F. & F. 731.) In this case Erle C.J. allowed the dog to be brought into court in charge of his keeper. The dog was afterwards liberated and the jury inspected him at close quarters. In his summing up the Chief Justice said that they might form an opinion as to the disposition of the animal in question partly from their

7—2

knowledge of dogs and from their observance of the
animal when produced for inspection[1].

Where a dog was shown to have exhibited a
ferocious disposition by invariably rushing out of his
kennel when any stranger passed and by jumping up
as far as his chain would allow him, barking and trying
to bite, this was held sufficient even in the absence
of evidence that the animal had bitten any person
before the doing of the injury which was the subject-
matter of the action.   One of the tenants of the yard
in which the dog was kept, who spoke to the savage
disposition of the animal, also said he had complained
to defendants about it and told them that the dog
should be more closely secured; but on cross-examination he would not say whether this was before or
after the injury had been inflicted upon the plaintiff.
The defendants admitted that the dog was purchased
for the protection of their premises.   The Court held
there was evidence to go to the jury that the animal
possessed a ferocious disposition towards mankind and
that the defendants were aware of the fact. (Worth v.
Gilling [1866], L.R. 2 C.P. 1.)   The allegation that
the animal was accustomed to bite mankind was added
at nisi prius by way of amendment to the declaration.

It now seems to be well-settled law that to establish
liability it is not necessary to show that the animal
has, to the knowledge of its owner, actually committed
or attempted to commit an act of harm of the kind

[1] The reporter adds a note on the importance of the case as
throwing some light upon the provisions of the Common Law
Procedure Act 1854, sec. 58, with regard to the inspection by the
jury or witnesses of property material to the determination of the
question in dispute.

which is the subject-matter of the action. It is sufficient to prove that the animal had a propensity to commit such an act, and that its owner knew this. A modern instance of the facts requisite to support the alleged vicious propensity of the animal occurs in the case of Barnes v. Lucille ([1907], 96 L.T. 680). A bitch, which at the time had three pups, had made frequent efforts to enter a workroom in which the plaintiff, an apprentice milliner, was employed by the owners of the animal. The occupants of the workroom were in considerable fear of the defendants' dogs getting in, and ultimately the bitch did get in and bit the plaintiff. The defendants' manager admitted in evidence that the dogs were of uncertain temper; and in correspondence passing previously to the commencement of the action he pointed out that the fact that the bitch had pups at the time of the accident might be the reason why the animal attacked the plaintiff. The judge held that there was no sufficient evidence of any previous biting, but that it was sufficient to find, as he did find, that the defendants knew the dog had a propensity to bite people, and that defendants took no precaution to prevent it getting into the room. He also referred to the evidence that since the accident such precautions had been taken, and he held this to be material as showing that the defendants knew precautions ought to be taken.

On appeal the Divisional Court held that there was evidence upon which the judge might come to the conclusion at which he had arrived. Darling J. there said: "It is a misapprehension on the part of many people to suppose that in order to make the owner of a dog liable the dog must have actually bitten someone before. Nor do I think it necessary to show that the dog has attempted to bite somebody.... What is necessary is that there should be evidence that the dog is a ferocious dog, which means that he would be likely to bite without provocation. There are many dogs which will bite other animals which are perfectly harmless with human beings. I do not think, further, that in order to make the owner of a dog liable that the dog must be always and invariably ferocious. If the owner knows that at certain periods the dog is ferocious, then he has knowledge that at those times the dog is of such a character that he ought to take care of it. If a man knows that a bitch which is ordinarily amiable is ferocious when she has pups, and people go near her, I think he has knowledge that at such times she is of a ferocious character, and in these circumstances he ought to shut her up and prevent her getting at people while she is ferocious, although the ferocity of the dog's character is intermittent."

A somewhat similar case of injury arose in Clinton v. Lyons (ante, p. 75), where a cat, which had kittened, bit and injured a dog and its owner who was carrying it at the time. It was held in that case that there was no sufficient evidence to prove that a cat with kittens is likely to do mischief to such a person. The judgments in the case are far from clear. The term "ferae naturae" is used to denote a dangerous animal, and it is assumed that an animal becomes 'dangerous,' so as to be the subject of the absolute duty, only when it is dangerous to mankind. This confusion lies at the root of both the judgments delivered. The actual decision in the case on the points raised can be supported by reference to the principles laid down in previous pages of this work. But it is difficult to understand the reasons given.

4. (1) By statute, the owner of a dog is liable in damages for injury done to any cattle by that dog; and it is not necessary for the person seeking such damages to show a previous mischievous propensity in the dog, or the owner's knowledge of such previous propensity, or to show that the injury was attributable to neglect on the part of the owner.

(2) Where any such injury has been done by a dog, the occupier of any house or premises where the dog was kept or permitted to live or remain at the time of the injury is presumed to be the owner of the dog and is liable for the injury unless he proves that he was not the owner of the dog at that time: provided that where there are more occupiers than one in any house or premises let in separate apartments, or lodgings, or otherwise, the occupier of that particular part of the house or premises in which the dog has been kept or permitted to live or remain at the time of the injury is presumed to be the owner of the dog.

(3) If the damages claimed under the above rules do not exceed five pounds they may be recovered under the Summary Jurisdiction Acts as a civil debt.

(4) In the above rules the expression "cattle" includes horses, mules, asses, sheep, goats and swine.

Cases have already been cited in which it appears that it is a vicious or mischievous act for a dog to attack and injure sheep, cattle, horses and other animals. But by the Dogs Act 1906 ([6 Edw. VII c. 32] repealing and re-enacting with some alterations the Dogs Act 1865 [28 & 29 Vict. c. 60]) a beneficial alteration of the law is made. The substance of the provisions of the present Act, as far as they are material to this work, are set out in the principles at the head of this section. Under the Act the principle of absolute liability is adopted, all that need be proved being the ownership and the injury.

In Lewis v. Jones ([1884], 49 J.P. 198) a case brought under the provisions of the earlier Act, appellant's dog was seen with another dog on a Welsh mountain in the act of worrying two lambs. The same day the shepherd found near the place four lambs dead, and the next day ten more. On the hearing of a case stated by justices the Court held that the evidence was sufficient to enable the justices to draw the inference that the dog had been concerned in the killing of the lambs subsequently found dead and justified them in ordering the appellant to pay part of the value of the whole loss.

In Campbell v. Wilkinson ([1909] 43 I.L.T. 237) the plaintiff was driving home two foals along the public road past defendant's farm when a young dog belonging to defendant rushed out of his house and barked at the foals. The foals broke away from the plaintiff's brother, who was in charge of them, and were not recovered until the next day. Both foals subsequently died from injuries received during the night. It was held that this was not an 'injury' within section 1 of the Dogs Act 1906. From this case it seems also that the Act does not exclude the defence of contributory negligence.

The fact that plaintiff's cattle were trespassing on defendant's land at the time of the injury is no defence to the action. (Grange v. Silcock [1897], 13 T.L.R. 565.) This was a case on section 1 of the Act of 1865, but the same principle, it is conceived, would apply to the present Act. Mr Justice Collins there said that the words of the statute were absolute. There was no express exception in favour of a dog which caught sheep trespassing. Nevertheless he thought it would be possible to conceive cases which would render it necessary to read some qualification into the words of the section. Thus if a wild bull escaped into a man's field and a dog used for driving it out bit the bull, it might be allowable. Words of this sort might then have to be deemed to be introduced into the section unless some legal justification for employing the dog be shown. But that question did not arise in the case he had to consider; the dog could not be in a better position than its master; he had no right to kill trespassers but only to use such violence as was necessary to remove them. The dog was not assisting his master, and therefore the case fell within the absolute words of the statute.

The second rule above stated practically reproduces sub-section 2 of the first section of the Act of 1906. This sub-section is not so wide as the corresponding section of the earlier Act. There, the person sought to be made responsible could escape liability only by proving that he was not the owner at the time of the injury "and that such dog was kept or permitted to live or remain in the said house or premises without his sanction or knowledge."

The effect of sub-section 2 of the Act of 1906 is most obscure. Supposing the occupier discharges the burden of proof cast upon him, who is responsible for the injury? Mr Salmond (Torts, p. 394) suggests several alternative answers to this question and indicates the problems which arise thereon. The question would form an excellent subject for debate.

The fourth rule reproduces section 7 of the Act. The earlier Act applied only to sheep and cattle, but in the case of Wright v. Pearson ([1869], L.R. 4 Q.B. 582) the term "cattle" was construed as including horses.

To the above remarks on the statutory provisions it may be added (although this is somewhat outside the purview of this treatise) that by section 1 (4) where a dog is proved to have injured cattle or chased sheep, it may be dealt with under section 2 of the Dogs Act 1871 as a "dangerous dog"; that is to say, a Court of Summary Jurisdiction may order that it be kept under proper control or destroyed, the penalty for non-

compliance with such order being a fine not exceeding
twenty shillings for every day during which such
non-compliance continues. The order for destruction
may be made in the first instance without giving the
owner the option of keeping the dog under proper
control. Again, by section 2 the Board of Agriculture
and Fisheries is empowered to make orders under the
Diseases of Animals Act 1894, section 22, with a view
to the prevention of worrying of cattle, for preventing
dogs or any class of dogs from straying during all or
any of the hours between sunset and sunrise, which
orders may provide that any dog in respect of which an
offence is being committed against the orders may be
seized and treated as a 'stray dog.'

5. Knowledge of a servant or agent is
knowledge of the owner of the animal if the
latter has delegated to his servant or agent
either:

(1) the carrying on of his business; or

(2) the control of the animal which caused
the injury.

Knowledge of the vicious or mischievous propensity
of the animal may be brought home to the owner
through the medium of an agent. Actual notice to
the agent is essential. But the evidence of this may
be such as would be sufficient in law in the case of the
owner himself.

It is not sufficient to show that *any* person in the
employment of the owner has a knowledge of the
dangerous propensity of the animal. In Stiles v.

Cardiff Steam Navigation Co. ([1864], 33 L.J. (Q.B.)
310) the defendants were a company, and the evidence
adduced to prove the scienter was that on some former
occasion some of the servants of the defendants had
heard, and one of them had seen, the animal (in this
case also, a dog) spring upon and bite someone else,
but those servants had no control over the affairs of
the defendant Company or over the dog; and this
was held to be insufficient to charge the defendants.
Crompton J. there said: "I quite agree that the knowledge of a servant representing his masters and acting
within the scope of their delegated authority may be
competent to affect his masters with that knowledge.
But is it found in this case that any such persons had
knowledge, persons competent to bind the defendants
by their admissions?...for such evidence is in the
nature of an admission.   No doubt there must be some
such person; for there must have been someone on
the premises to control the business of the defendants.
It would have been sufficient to show knowledge in
the manager or some person having the control of the
yard.   I had some doubt whether the knowledge must
not be brought home to some person who kept and had
care of the dog, and had power to put an end to the
keeping of it; but perhaps it would be enough if he
had the care of the dog.   But all that is found is that
some persons who appear rather to have had the care
of horses had seen or had heard that the dog had
bitten a person before.   It is more like the case of
a gardener or a cook hearing that their mistress's
lap-dog was given to bite; and I think that the evidence
wholly fails to bring home the knowledge to any person

whose knowledge in point of law would be that of the defendants.''

In an action for damages for an injury caused by the bite of a dog, a witness deposed that information that the dog had bitten another person had been given to the defendant's wife four years previously. She, being called as a witness, denied ever having received any notice of the kind. Defendant's wife was accustomed to assist her husband in his business of a milkman. The Court held that the evidence was slight but sufficient evidence of scienter to be submitted to a jury. The complaint of the previous injury upon which the scienter was based had been made on the premises to the wife, had the character of a message, and was delivered to the first person who seemed to have authority to receive such a message. (Gladman v. Johnson [1867], 15 L.T. (N.S.) 476.) In the case of Miller v. Kimbray ([1867], 16 L.T. (N.S.) 360) a doubt was expressed at nisi prius whether the converse would hold good, i.e. whether notice to a husband, simpliciter, would render his wife liable. The facts of the case were as follows: The plaintiff had attended at defendant's house to pay her rent and was attacked and bitten by defendant's dog as she was passing through the defendant's yard. A witness stated that he had been bitten by the same dog some years previously and that he had brought an action in consequence; that that was during the lifetime of defendant's husband (who at the time the present action was brought had been dead for some considerable time) and that the witness's complaint had been made to the husband. Mellor J. did not think that a notice to the husband

should be taken to be a notice to the wife, as a man
might be told many things that he never communicated
to his wife. After consulting the other judges his
lordship said he would leave it to the jury to say
whether, under all the circumstances, they thought
that the defendant knew, or must have known, that
the dog was of a fierce and savage nature. A verdict
was given for the plaintiff.

Presumably the action mentioned as having been
brought by the witness in this case was brought against
the defendant's husband; though of course it might
have been brought against husband and wife together.
Even in the former case the very fact of the action
having been brought against the husband would seem
to be evidence of knowledge on the part of the wife
sufficient at least to have been left to the jury. There
could hardly be any dispute as to her knowledge in
the latter case. On the other hand, if the action had
been brought against the husband alone, it may have
been brought against him as owner of the dog, and a
notice to him as owner should not, unless actually
communicated, adversely affect a person who became
owner subsequently. (Cf. Mason v. Keeling, ante,
p. 80.) No question of. delegated authority seems to
have arisen in this case.

Apparently notice to defendant's infant son (aged
eleven) is sufficient to fix the defendant with the
scienter. (Elliott v. Longden [1901], 17 T.L.R. 648.)
But note that the action in this case was brought
under the provisions of section 1 of the Dogs Act 1865.

The question of constructive knowledge was discussed at great length in the case of Applebee v. Percy

([1874], L.R. 9 C.P. 647), another case of dog bite.
Here, two witnesses proved that they had been
attacked by the animal on previous occasions and had
gone to the defendant's public-house and made complaint to two persons who were behind the bar serving
customers. There was no evidence that these complaints had been communicated to the defendant; nor
was it shown that either of the two men spoken to had
the general management of the defendant's business
or had the care of the dog. It was held by Lord
Coleridge C.J. and Keating J. (Brett J. diss.) that there
was evidence of scienter to go to the jury. The view
of Brett J. differed from that of the majority of the
Court upon the ground that the barmen, to whom complaint of the previous injuries had been made, had no
duty in relation to defendant's business other than that
of serving customers and of receiving the price fixed
by their master. They were not persons who stood
in the place of their master and to whom the general
control of the business was delegated in the master's
absence. "To say that the knowledge of a wife or a
servant is the knowledge of the husband or the master,
irrespectively of the particular position or duties of
the party in relation to the husband's or the master's
business, would, in my judgment, be to uproot all
one's notions of commercial dealings and to dispense
altogether with the scienter in cases of this sort."
Keating J. was of opinion, on the authority of Gladman
v. Johnson (ante, p. 109), that the notice had been given
to persons carrying on the defendant's business on his
premises so far as it could be carried on by them alone,
that the persons in question had authority to receive

it, that under such circumstances it was their duty to communicate it to their master and that it was not too much to conclude, as a matter of fact, that they did so communicate it. Lord Coleridge delivered a judgment to the same effect and pointed out that it was not a question of the weight of evidence but whether such evidence was given. "The matter may, I think, be put in either of two ways. In the first place, it may be said that the persons to whom the notice was given were in the position of managers of the defendant's business; not managers in the strict and full sense suggested by my Brother Brett, but, as in Gladman v. Johnson, persons interested, in the absence of their employer, with the conduct of his business; and that a notice to them of the vicious and ferocious nature of a dog kept about the premises where the business was so managed or conducted by them was, upon principle and upon authority, evidence fit to be submitted to the jury of a notice to their employer. Or it may be put upon another ground, viz. that suggested in Stiles v. Cardiff Steam Navigation Co. (ante, p. 108) and Baldwin v. Casella ([1872], L.R. 7 Exch. 325), that where a certain business or the performance of a certain duty is deputed to a servant, a notice to the servant so acting is a notice to the master, because he has placed the servant in his stead to represent him quoad that particular business or duty. ...It seems to me that there was evidence in this case upon which the jury ought to have been asked whether they thought the persons to whom the notice was given were persons who stood in such a relation to the defendant as to make it their duty to communicate it to him. It appears to me that all the ingredients for forming a judgment in that case exist here, and that the persons to whom the notice was given might reasonably be presumed to have had authority to receive such notice and to have made it their duty to convey it to the defendant and that they did in fact do so."

In Baldwin v. Casella, cited in the last case, the dog by which the plaintiff was bitten was kept in a stable of the defendant's situated in a mews, and was under the care and control of the defendant's coachman, who lived there. There was evidence which satisfied the jury that the dog had some time previously knocked down the plaintiff and scratched him and that this was known to the coachman. To prove the vicious temper of the animal evidence was given that on two previous occasions it had attacked persons passing through the mews, but this was not known either to the defendant or his coachman. The injury to the plaintiff also was not known to the defendant, who supposed the dog to be harmless, and allowed it to play with his own children. Mr Baron Cleasby directed the jury that if the coachman knew of the previous attack by the dog, his knowledge was the knowledge of his master, and that the defendant was liable. The jury found a verdict for the plaintiff. Upon motion for a new trial on the ground of misdirection, the Court of Exchequer approved the ruling. Martin B. said: "I think the direction of the learned judge was right. The dog was kept in the defendant's stable and the defendant's coachman was appointed to keep it; the coachman knew that the dog was

mischievous, and it is immaterial whether he communicated the fact to his master or not; his knowledge
was the knowledge of his master." The judgment of
Bramwell B. rested upon wider grounds. "It appears
to be the rule of law, that the possibility of loss and
injury arising to others from things which are likely
to be dangerous raises, on the part of those who have
them under their control, a duty to inform themselves
about them. . . . So all dogs may be mischievous; and
therefore a man who keeps a dog is bound either to
have it under his own observation and inspection, or,
if not, to appoint someone under whose observation
and inspection it may be. The defendant has appointed
his coachman to that duty; the coachman knew of the
mischievous propensities of the dog; and his knowledge
is the knowledge of the master."

According to the view of the learned judge it
would seem that the mere fact of keeping a dog may be
held to involve a duty of using due care to ascertain
whether it has, or even is likely to have, a mischievous
or vicious nature.

The fact that a domestic servant who was employed
by the defendant had seen or had heard that the dog
had bitten a person before, is not sufficient to fix the
defendant with constructive notice, if the servant had
not control of the animal. Thus in Colget v. Norrish
([1886], 2 T.L.R. 471) an attempt to fix the defendant
with a constructive knowledge failed under the following
circumstances: A postman was delivering letters at
defendant's house and when the front door was opened
defendant's collie dog flew at the postman and bit his
leg. In the action for damages which the plaintiff

brought in the County Court there was evidence that complaints of the ferocity of the dog had been made to defendant's domestic servant. Upon this the County Court Judge found that although these complaints were not communicated to the defendant or his wife, the communications to the servant were sufficient evidence of scienter in the defendant, as it was the servant's duty to tell her master of them. On appeal to the Divisional Court a difference of opinion occurred, Mathew J. thinking that there should be a new trial, and A. L. Smith J. holding that judgment should be given for the defendant. A. L. Smith J. withdrew his judgment, and the order for a new trial stood, the defendants having leave to appeal. The Court of Appeal allowed the appeal and ordered judgment to be entered for the defendant on the ground that the County Court Judge had found as a fact that no complaints had reached defendant as to the dog having bitten anyone or as to its being ferocious. And per Lopes L.J. notice to the domestic servant could not be said to be notice to the master.

At first sight it may seem difficult to distinguish this case from Baldwin v. Casella. But there the actual care and control of the dog had been delegated to the coachman, which was not the case here. Again, in this case it was expressly found as a fact that defendant had no notice.

In Cleverton v. Uffernel ([1887], 3 T.L.R. 509) an action was brought to recover damages for injuries sustained by the plaintiff who had been bitten by defendant's dog whilst in the bar of the defendant's public-house. At the trial the jury found in answer

8—2

to three questions put to them (1) that the dog was dangerous to mankind, (2) that the defendant did not know it, and (3) that one Russell, defendant's brother-in-law, and employed as defendant's potman, did know it. The second answer was directed by the learned judge (Denman J.), who held that there was no evidence against the defendant that he personally knew the dog's disposition; but on the whole findings his lordship left the plaintiff to move for judgment. On cross motions for judgment and for a new trial the Court (Day and Wills J.J.) ordered a new trial on the ground of misdirection, Mr Justice Day observing that the learned judge was wrong in directing the jury to find for the defendant on the question whether he had knowledge, and that the first question was whether Russell had charge of the dog so that his knowledge would be constructive knowledge in the defendant.

6. The general conditions of liability being present, it is immaterial (subject to the exceptions hereafter mentioned) whether the act of harm complained of causes injury to the person or damage to property (including other animals), or whether it is committed on the premises where the animal is kept, or on the premises of the plaintiff, or on the highway or elsewhere.

Wherever the general conditions of liability which have been laid down in previous pages are fulfilled, and there is no specific ground of defence, the absolute duty arises irrespective of the object of the injury or

the place where it is committed. There is no need to
enter into a detailed illustration of this. Sufficient
instances have already been given to show that the
nature or character of the object of the harm does not
affect liability.

With regard to the place of the injury, in Filburn's
case the harm was received on defendant's premises,
in Read v. Edwards on the plaintiff's land, and in Cox
v. Burbidge on the highway.

It is to be noted that although a person may be
liable for acts of harm committed by his animals
whilst they are trespassers, those acts may or may not
be natural to the animal to commit. In the latter
case there may be alternative remedies. If the harm
received be within the rules as to remoteness of damage,
the owner may be liable in trespass. If the scienter
be proved, the owner is subject to the absolute liability.
On these points the reader is referred to page 38 et seq.

7. The absolute liability for harm caused
by animals is excluded in the following
circumstances:

(*a*) where the injury was caused by vis
major or the act of God. Sed quaere.

(*b*) where the immediate cause of the
injury complained of was the act of a third
person.

(*c*) where the plaintiff suffers by his own
default or brings the injury upon himself; or
where he, knowing of the risk of harm, voluntarily undertakes it. Volenti non fit injuria.

(*d*) where the plaintiff, at the time of the injury complained of, was trespassing upon the premises where the animal was kept.

It remains to consider whether there are any exceptions to the rule of strict responsibility for injury caused by ferocious or mischievous animals or by harmless or domestic animals which are known to have vicious or mischievous propensities.

If reference be made to the principle underlying the cases of which Rylands v. Fletcher is the generalisation, the principle to which the present subject is so often (and, it is submitted, wrongly) referred, it will be found that there are at least two or three well-defined exceptions to liability which might, at first sight, have application here. Thus the rule in Rylands v. Fletcher has been decided by the Court of Appeal not to apply to damage of which the immediate cause is the act of God, that is to say, to damage which is the result of some natural occurrence which could not reasonably be foreseen or anticipated. Whether the damage falls into this category is a question of fact. (Nichols v. Marsland [1875], L.R. 10 Exch. 255.)

Again, the general principle has no application where the immediate cause of damage is the act of a stranger—(Box v. Jubb [1879], 4 Exch. Div. 76)—or where the injured person brings the injury upon himself.

Do these, or other similar exceptions, apply to the liability for wrongs committed by animals? Apparently exceptions to the liability do in fact exist. In May v. Burdett (ante, p. 58) Lord Denman C.J. said:

"Whoever keeps an animal accustomed to attack and bite mankind, with knowledge that it is so accustomed, is prima facie liable in an action on the case at the suit of any person attacked and injured by the animal, without any averment of negligence or default in the securing or taking care of it." If it is a prima facie liability, exceptions must exist. What are those exceptions?

In a later part of his judgment in the same case, Lord Denman suggests one possible exception: "It may be that, if the injury was solely occasioned by the wilfulness of the plaintiff after warning, that may be a ground of defence, by plea in confession and avoidance: but it is unnecessary to give any opinion as to this; for we think that the declaration is good upon the face of it, and shows a prima facie liability in the defendant." It is proposed to defer the consideration of this suggested exception until later.

Vis major or the act of God would seem to be no excuse, but the question is doubtful. That it was no excuse was evidently the opinion of the Court of Exchequer expressed in the judgment of the Court delivered by Bramwell B. in Nichols v. Marsland (supra). It was there held that a man who stores water on his own land and who uses all reasonable care to keep it safely is not liable to be sued for an escape of the water which injures his neighbour, if the escape be caused by an agency beyond his control. But the judgment distinguished the case from the case of the keeping of a wild or savage animal, and Bramwell B. went on to say: "I am by no means sure if a man kept a tiger, and lightning broke his chain, and he got loose and did mischief, that the man who kept him would not be liable." If this is the true view of the law, then a wrong resulting from the keeping of such an animal affords an instance, and possibly the only instance in the law of tort, where not even vis major is an excuse. The matter was also incidentally considered in the Court of Appeal in the case of Baker v. Snell ([1908] 2 K.B. 825), where the dictum of Bramwell B. was cited with approval by Cozens-Hardy M.R.

Secondly, does the fact that the injury was brought about by the intervening voluntary act of a third person afford an exception to the rules of liability? This was the main question which arose for solution in the case of Baker v. Snell (supra). In that case, the defendant, a publican, kept on his premises a dog which he knew to be a savage animal. He usually kept the dog chained up during the day, but his barman had instructions to let it out for a run each morning and to bring it back and tie it up before the other servants came downstairs. One morning the barman brought the dog back while the plaintiff and another barmaid were at breakfast. He brought it into the kitchen and said: "I bet the dog won't bite anyone," and added, "Go it, Bob"; whereupon the dog bit the plaintiff. Upon these facts the County Court Judge nonsuited the plaintiff on the ground that this was a wilful and malicious act on the part of the barman and was an assault by him. The Divisional Court (Channell and Sutton J.J.) set aside the judgment and ordered a new trial of the action. Channell J., after quoting the dictum of Bramwell B. (ante, p. 119), expressed the opinion that although it goes some way

to solving the question whether or not the liability of
the owner extends to rendering him liable for injury
done by a dog owing to the voluntary act of a third
person, yet he did not think that it could extend to
making the owner liable for the act of a third person
for whom the owner is in no way responsible; and he
went on to put the following case: "Suppose a dog is
placed in a house to protect the premises, and a thief
comes in; there can be no doubt that if he were bitten
by the dog he would have no cause of action. (This is
the exception dealt with in the fourth place.) But
suppose the thief were followed by a policeman, and the
thief released the dog and set it at the policeman, and
the dog bit him, I do not think that the policeman
would have any cause of action against the owner of
the dog, because the injury would be due to the act of
a third person for whose conduct the owner was in no
sense liable. But in the present case the person to
whose act the injury was due was the servant of the
defendant and the person to whom in point of fact
he had entrusted the dog." ([1908], 77 L.J. (K.B.) 727.)
He went on to hold that there was evidence from
which a jury might infer that the act of the servant
was done in neglect of his duty as custodian of the
dog, and that his master was therefore liable. He
thought, too, that it might be that, if the facts had
been left to a jury, the jury would have found that
the dog bit the plaintiff by reason of its savage disposition, and not in consequence of any inducement
by the barman.

Mr Salmond in dealing with the "very unsatis-
factory case of Baker v. Snell" (at page 392 of his

treatise on the law of torts) suggests that the case
might have been decided in favour of the defendant
on the ground of the doctrine of common employment.
That doctrine is at bottom an application of the
principle expressed in the maxim "volenti non fit
injuria," but it is difficult to see how that principle
could have been applied in this case. The risk of
injury from the dog could not be said to be a risk
incidental to the service. (Cf. Mansfield v. Baddeley
[1876], 34 L.T. 696.)

Mr Justice Sutton was of opinion that, as the gist
of such an action is the keeping of the animal after
knowledge of its vicious propensity, the owner was
liable for any injury caused by the animal in all circumstances, except where a plaintiff by his own conduct
had brought the injury upon himself.

The Court of Appeal (Cozens-Hardy M.R., Farwell
and Kennedy L.J.J.) held that the case ought to have
been left to the jury and that there must be a new
trial. But whilst the Master of the Rolls and Lord
Justice Farwell thought that the defendant was
responsible notwithstanding the intervening voluntary
act of a third person, Lord Justice Kennedy held that
the prima facie liability of the owner in such case does
not extend to injury brought about by such intervening act, at any rate if the act be one of a criminal
nature. The judgments are worthy of a careful
perusal, as they all three differ in detail as a result of a
different conception of the nature of the liability.
It is preferred here to adopt the judgment of the
Master of the Rolls as being the most sound exposition
of the law.

After stating and illustrating the absolute duty to prevent harm resulting from the keeping of an animal whose nature is ferocious or of an animal of a class not generally ferocious but which is known by the owner to be dangerous in fact, the learned judge adverted to the case of Nichols v. Marsland and quoted Mr Baron Bramwell's dictum, already cited, as going to show that the act of God or vis major is no excuse. He then proceeded to say: "That case came before the Court of Appeal, where Lord Justice Mellish delivered the judgment of the Court. He said: 'The ordinary rule of law is that when the law creates a duty and the party is disabled from performing it without any default of his own, by the act of God, or the King's enemies, the law will excuse him; but when a party by his own contract creates a duty, he is bound to make it good notwithstanding any accident by inevitable necessity. We can see no good reason why that rule should not be applied to the case before us. The duty of keeping the water in and preventing its escape is a duty imposed by the law, and not one created by contract. If, indeed, the making a reservoir was a wrongful act in itself, it might be right to hold that a person could not escape from the consequences of his own wrongful act.' If it is true, as I think it is, that it is a wrongful act to keep an animal which is known to be dangerous, that is an authority, not merely of the Court of Exchequer, but also of the Court of Appeal, that the person so keeping it is liable for the consequences of his wrongful act, even though the immediate cause of damage is the act of a third party." ([1908], 77 L.J. (K.B.) 1093.) The question has already been considered as to whether the keeping an animal which is known to be dangerous is in itself a wrongful act[1].

In the course of his judgment in this case Farwell L.J. in terms laid down that the act of keeping the animal is a wrongful act and involves liability for the consequences under whatever circumstances arising. But he qualified his proposition almost immediately: "The wrong is in keeping the fierce beast; and the person who chooses to keep it is responsible for the injury arising from his own wrongful act, unless the injury was due to the plaintiff's own default or (possibly) to vis major or the act of God: these are the only exceptions, as appears from Lord Blackburn's judgment in Fletcher v. Rylands, and it is to these that he refers when, just before, he speaks of the prima facie liability of the defendant."

It is submitted that the judgment of Lord Blackburn (then Blackburn J.) is no authority for saying that vis major or the act of God is an exception to the liability of the person who keeps such an animal.

The judgment of the Court of Exchequer Chamber in Fletcher v. Rylands was quoted by Lord Cairns with approval when the same case came before the House of Lords. The terms of the judgment have already been noticed (see pages 48 and 49), and it has been seen that although they may be an excellent exposition of the law as to the escape and trespass of cattle or domestic or ordinarily harmless animals, they have nothing to do with injuries by dangerous animals, or

---

[1] The reader is referred to page 66 et seq., where authorities on both sides are quoted.

by animals known to have dangerous proclivities. Be
that as it may, attention need be directed only to the
fact that we are now dealing—and the case of Baker v.
Snell deals—not with the escape and trespass of
animals, but with the case of harm caused by the
actual keeping of animals. It was never alleged in
that case, or in May v. Burdett, or in Jackson v.
Smithson, or in many other similar cases, that the
harm was caused by the animal's escape or trespass:
it was caused while the owner *kept* the animal, i.e.
while he had the actual control of it, and the judgments
were all based on that fact, and that was held to be
sufficient to found the action. The truth is, as was
premised earlier in this treatise, that the cases of injury
by animals, apart from trespass, belong to a wider
field of responsibility than that of which the principles
are generalised in Rylands v. Fletcher. Hence, what
may be exceptions to the rule in Rylands v. Fletcher
cannot, on that account, be held to be exceptions to
the rule of absolute liability for harm resulting from
the keeping of animals.

There appears little to be said concerning the
decision of Kennedy L.J. He draws the inference
from the case of Jackson v. Smithson (ante, p. 84) that
there is nothing wrongful in the act of keeping a
dangerous animal. He also refers to the introduction
of the terms "prima facie liability" in the judgment
of Lord Denman in May v. Burdett and draws
the inference that liability does not extend to
damage directly brought about by the intervening
voluntary act of a third person. Sed non sequitur,
and Lord Denman himself in the next following

passage of his judgment indicated the exception he had in mind.

Now comes the consideration of the third suggested exception, namely, where the plaintiff suffers by his own default, or brings the injury upon himself, or as Lord Denman puts it, where "the injury was solely occasioned by the wilfulness of the plaintiff after warning."

The defence is practically the equivalent of Contributory Negligence, but that term is not used here, as it assumes to some extent that the wrong to the plaintiff is based on negligence, which, of course, it is not.

Where defendant, who was the owner of some zebras, had kept his animals securely fastened up in a stable, he was held, by the unanimous judgment of the Court of Appeal, not liable in an action for damages brought by a person who had gone into the stable to stroke one of the animals, and whilst doing so had received injury. Lord Justice A. L. Smith in the course of his judgment there said it was conceded that a zebra was a dangerous animal, and that by law a man who kept a dangerous animal must do so at his peril, and that if any damage resulted, then, apart from any question of negligence, he was liable for the damage. But that was subject to this—that the person who complained of damage must not have brought the injury on himself. Where the plaintiff did something which he had no business to do—e.g. by meddling, as the plaintiff in this case had done—then the defendant was not liable. After quoting the remarks by Lord Esher in Filburn's case on this point, his Lordship

went on to say that the action could not be maintained
on the common law liability. The plaintiff then set
up a claim for negligence, viz. that the door was not
kept locked, and that there was no keeper at hand.
The evidence showed that the door had been shut, but
had got opened. If the plaintiff had been kicked
while walking along the stable an action might have
lain, but the plaintiff went into the stall and meddled
with the animal. Even if the fact of the door being
open was an invitation to go into the stable, it was not
an invitation to stroke the animals. In his opinion
there was no evidence to go to the jury and judgment
must be entered for the defendant. (Marlor v. Ball
[1900], 16 T.L.R. 239.)

In a recent Scottish case it was held that it is not
contributory negligence to pat a strange dog in the
street, the dog happening to be a vicious dog and
biting the plaintiff. (Gordon v. Mackenzie [1912],
2 Scots Law Times, p. 334.) "The public are entitled
to expect that a dog that is allowed to wander about a
street unattended is not a dangerous dog; and I cannot
hold that a person who, when a dog approaches him,
pats it or puts out his hand to pat it, either from
friendliness or it may be in order to conciliate it, is
guilty of contributory negligence" (The Lord Justice-
Clerk at p. 335). (Cf. Smith v. Pelah, 2 Str. 1264.)
A case which is similar to the foregoing arises
where a person, knowing of the risk of harm from the
animal, voluntarily undertakes it. This exception from
liability is usually shortly referred to by the maxim
'volenti non fit injuria.'

In Mansfield v. Baddeley ([1876] 34 L.T. 696)

defendant was a dressmaker and the plaintiff a work-
woman in her employ. The defendant kept a dog
which was in her house when plaintiff took the situation.
It was admitted on both sides that the dog was a
savage brute, and the plaintiff was aware of its disposition. The plaintiff went one day into the kitchen,
at the request of the defendant, when the dog, which
was generally tied up, rushed from under the table and
bit her leg. At the trial of an action for damages for
the injury the case was left to the jury, who found for
the plaintiff. Subsequently the judge directed a nonsuit on the point of law raised at the trial that the
plaintiff was a servant and knew that the dog was a
savage dog and that the action could not be maintained.
On the argument of a rule to set aside the ruling of
the judge, the Court (Cleasby B. and Grove J.) gave
judgment for the plaintiff, on the ground that she
could not be said to have taken the risk of harm upon
herself when she knew the dog was generally tied up,
and she went downstairs believing that it was so tied
up. But Cleasby B. said : "If the plaintiff, knowing
that the dog was of a savage disposition, had gone of
his (sic) own accord to the place where the dog was
about loose, with a knowledge that it was there, in
that case I should hold that she took the chance of the
dog being in a humour to bite her, and could not
recover." Similarly, Grove J.: "It is said that the
plaintiff knew of this dog when she entered the service
of the defendant. No doubt she cannot recover for
risks incidental to the service. I think that this risk
is not incidental to the service, nor do I see anything in
the conduct of the plaintiff which would disentitle her

to recover. If the plaintiff when she entered her employment knew the character of the dog, and that in the ordinary course of her employment she would have to go by the place where it was tied up, it might perhaps be said she took the risk. But here she was asked to do something which was no part of her service, in fact a mere good-natured act, it being something ultra her service to go to the kitchen. The dog then rushes out and bites her. Such a risk was not incidental to the service, nor one which by her conduct she has undertaken to bear."

Turning to the fourth exception mentioned above, the case of the harm occurring to a trespasser, in an old case, Brock v. Copeland ([1794] 1 Esp. 203), where action was brought to recover for the bite of a dog, it was ruled that if the dog were kept on defendant's premises and the injury received in consequence of the plaintiff imprudently going there, the action cannot be maintained. The defendant was a carpenter, and the dog was kept for the protection of his yard; the dog was tied up during the day (and was then very quiet and gentle) but was let loose at night. The plaintiff, who acted as defendant's foreman, went into the yard after it had been shut up for the night, and the dog bit and injured him. A nonsuit was entered. Lord Kenyon, in the course of his remarks, said that every man had a right to keep a dog for the protection of his yard or house and that the injury which an action of this nature was calculated to redress was, where the animal, known to be mischievous, was permitted to go at large, and the injury arose from the not securing the animal so as not to endanger or injure the public; that

N. B.   9

here the dog had been properly let loose and the injury
had arisen from the plaintiff's own fault in incautiously
going into defendant's yard after it had been shut up.
The report then goes on to say: "His lordship added
that in a former case, where in an action against a man
for keeping a mischievous bull, that had hurt the
plaintiff, it having appeared in evidence, that the
plaintiff was crossing a field of the defendant's where
the bull was kept and where he had received the
injury, the defendant's counsel contended, that the
plaintiff having gone there of his own head, and having
received the injury from his own fault, that an action
would not lie; but that it appearing also in evidence,
that there was a contest concerning a right of way over
this field, wherein the bull was kept, and that the
defendant had permitted several persons to go over it
as an open way, that he had ruled in that case, and
the Court of King's Bench had concurred in opinion
with him, that the plaintiff having gone into the
field, supposing that he had a right to go there, as over
a legal way, that he should not then be allowed to set
up in his defence, the right of keeping such an animal
there as in his own close, but that the action was
maintainable."

In Sarch v. Blackburn ([1830], 4 Car. & P. 297) the
plaintiff brought an action for damages for injury
received from the bite of a dog under the following
circumstances: The defendant carried on the business
of a milkman, and his sons that of a cow-keeper.
Defendant's dog was in a yard near some outbuildings
and was attached to its kennel by a chain about four
yards long. Over the kennel, nailed against the

palings, was a board, on which was painted in letters
three inches in length "Beware of the dog." The
plaintiff was unable to read. There were three en-
trances to the premises, two of which were more
private than the third and a person passing along either
of these might have occasion to approach the dog.
A witness proved that he had been bitten by the dog
previously and that this was known to defendant.
He admitted on cross-examination that the accident
occurred to him as he was passing along one of the
private ways through which he thought he had no
business to go. Chief Justice Tindal, in his remarks to
the jury, said: "You must show that the dog was
accustomed to bite, and that the defendant knew it,
before you can throw upon him the responsibility of
keeping it from doing so. If a man puts a dog in a
garden, walled all round, and a wrongdoer goes into
that garden, and is bitten, he cannot complain in a
Court of Justice of that which was brought upon him
by his own act....Undoubtedly a man has a right to
keep a fierce dog for the protection of his property, but
he has no right to put the dog in such a situation, in
the way of access to his house, that a person innocently
coming for a lawful purpose may be injured by it. I
think he has no right to place a dog so near to the
door of his house that any person coming to ask for
money, or on other business, might be bitten. And so
with respect to a footpath, though it be a private one, a
man has no right to put a dog with such a length of
chain, and so near that path, that he could bite a
person going along it. As to the notice, it does not
appear to me that a painted notice is sufficient, unless

9—2

the party is in such a situation in life as to be able to avail himself of it. It does not appear to me that this notice is sufficient so as to bar the action, if the plaintiff had any right at all to be on the spot, for it seems that he was not able to read."

Exception may be taken to the statements of Lord Kenyon and Tindal C.J. that a person has a right to keep a fierce dog for the protection of his premises. Perhaps what is meant is, that a person against whom the premises require protection—a person who wrongfully enters upon those premises—cannot be heard to complain that the keeping of such an animal is a wrongful act. It would seem that this is sufficiently shown from the words of the former when he says that the action lies where the injury arose from the not securing the animal so as not to endanger or injure the public. (It is submitted that there is nothing inconsistent here with the fact that an absolute duty is prescribed and not a duty of using care merely.) That Tindal C.J. means the same seems to be shown from the opening words of his statement, and by his test of inquiring whether, in the particular place, the means adopted by the defendant for securing the animal were sufficient, i.e. sufficient not to endanger or injure the public. It is not a question of degree, but a question of fact one way or the other. Unless some such explanation as this be accepted, then the dicta of the two judges must be taken as being inconsistent with and overruled by the decisions in the more recent cases. The manner in which the law distinguishes between a trespasser and a person coming upon premises on lawful business has been stated as

III] *other Animals, and Damage to Goods* 133

follows: "While, if a dog is known to be vicious, its owner is under an obligation to keep it in proper restraint, yet knowledge that it is a vicious dog does not impose an obligation on the owner's friends and acquaintances to stay away from his premises, and they are merely bound to exercise a reasonable amount of precaution. The owner is excepted from liability where the person injured was a trespasser, or where the dog was kept in the owner's own premises during the night to protect them....But on the other hand, it is no ground of defence that the dog was kept in premises during the day if it was kept in such a position that it could attack a person who calls at the premises on lawful business, whether of the owner or of the visitor." (21 Ir. Law Times 53.)

It is proposed to defer consideration of the position of persons who are injured by animals whilst they are on the premises of the owner of the animals by his invitation or as licensees. It seems preferable to treat of these matters in connection with the duty of a person who occupies premises which are rendered dangerous by reason of the keeping of dangerous animals thereon.

8. (1) The person who has kept a dangerous animal probably remains responsible for acts of harm committed by it even after it has escaped, provided it is one of a class which is not usually found at large in this country.

(2) If the animal is one of a class which usually enjoys a state of natural liberty in

this country, then, it is submitted, the responsibility ceases as soon as the animal has returned to its natural state sine animo revertendi.

The question of the duration of responsibility for the acts of a harmful animal is still a matter of conjecture. Upon principle, a person who keeps a tiger, a monkey or other animal which is not usually found at liberty in this country remains responsible after its escape for harm done by it at any time. The remarks of Lord Denman in May v. Burdett are wide enough to cover the case, and it would seem that the learned judge must have had it in contemplation at the time of delivering his judgment, for, in argument of that case, reference was made to a rule of the Civil law touching upon the matter. (Inst. IV. 9: "Si ursus fugit a domino et sic nocuit, non potest quondam dominus conveniri, quia desinit dominus esse, ubi fera evasit.") At any rate it is difficult to conceive any other rule than that above enunciated.

Where the animal is of a class usually found at large in this country it is suggested that the rule is different. If the animal escapes and regains its wild state, there is no good reason for holding its former keeper responsible for its acts in the future. The risk of harm from it is the same as from that of all members of its species which are at large and is a common danger which every person must incur. The temporary captivity of the animal has in no way affected the matter. A person who, for instance, lets a rat out of a trap, has not enhanced the common danger and should not therefore be responsible for the future actions of the animal. "If one kept a tame fox which gets loose and grows wild, he that kept him before shall not answer for the damage the fox doth after he hath lost him and he hath remained in his wild nature." (1 Ventr. 295. Opinion of Marsden J.) This opinion was doubted by Johnson J. in Brady v. Warren, though he gives no reasons. From the point of view of convenience, the second suggested rule is as necessary as the first.

SECTION II. *The duty to take care, and other obligations*

1. (1) A person who keeps an animal is liable for harm caused by it or through its instrumentality in any circumstances in which the law raises a duty of taking care in the control of the animal on the part of that person, and there has been a breach of that duty.

(2) Such person is liable for the natural and probable consequences of the breach of duty but not for an unexpected event.

It has been mentioned in a previous part of this treatise that the owner may be liable on the ground of negligence for harm committed through the instrumentality of the animal he owns. This liability may be altogether independent of (1) the strict responsibility for harm caused by the keeping of the animal, or (2) the absolute duty of preventing its trespass upon the lands of others.

The incidence of this duty of using due care and caution in practical affairs, is much more obvious in the case where the animal is under the actual personal control of the owner or his servant than in cases where there is no such physical control. A horse which is being ridden, a dog which is being led, cattle which are being driven, may, and often do cause harm which is directly and solely attributable to the absence of care on the part of the person riding, leading or driving. And these cases are so familiar to us, and so similar in principle, that little purpose is served in referring to more than a few instances.

Again, there are similar cases where the harm is more or less due to the nature or characteristics of the animal itself. For instance, horses or cattle in charge of a person on the highway may be known to be of uncertain temper or of a harmful disposition and likely to cause injury if special care to control them be not taken. In such cases a duty to use a proportionate amount of care and caution will arise; that is to say, an amount sufficient to guard against not only the ordinary risk of accident due to the act of the person having control of the animal, but also against the risk of harm caused by the spontaneous act of the animal itself. This must be a question of degree. Considerably more care must be used, for instance, in taking an unbroken horse through a crowded thoroughfare than in driving through such a place with a horse, which, though properly broken in, is a high-spirited animal. The points to be attended to in cases of this sort are first, the character of the animal, and secondly, the purposes for or the circumstances in which it was

used. In Mitchell v. Alestre ([1677], 2 Lev. 172)
defendants took two "ungovernable" horses into
Lincoln's Inn Fields, "a place where people are always
going to and fro about their business," and "eux
improvide incaute et absque debita consideratione
ineptitudinis loci there drove them to make them
tractable and fit them for a coach; and the horses,
because of their ferocity, became not to be managed,
ran upon the plaintiff and hurt and grievously wounded
him." The defendants were held liable although no
scienter was alleged and proved.

A further class of cases occurs where the animal
does harm as a result of external causes over which
the person in charge of it has no control, e.g. where a
horse, frightened by escaping steam at a railway
station, runs away. It is conceivable that a slightly
different principle might be applied here, namely, as
to whether it was negligence to bring the animal into
such a place where it was known that ill effects might
follow. Beyond noticing such matters as these, it is
not intended to deal with them here.

Even in many of the cases of injury by the spontaneous act of animals which were considered under
the heading of the absolute duty, the declarations in
the actions contained an alternative allegation of
negligence; and far from being valueless, the very
presence of such allegations denoted their utility and
efficacy. For, had the evidence which was to be
adduced in support of the allegation of the stricter duty
been deemed insufficient, the suitor might still have
relied upon the allegation of negligence and possibly
have succeeded. Indeed, in many cases of injury by

domestic or harmless animals, and particularly in the case of injury to cattle by dogs before the law received statutory amendment on this point, the difficulty of proving the scienter was so great that negligence was more often relied upon as the ground of liability. The two grounds may exist simultaneously upon the same facts, as is shown by the case of Card v. Case (ante, p. 69), and the reader is referred to the extracts from the judgments there quoted. It is sufficient to emphasise the fact that the Court has held in that, and in other similar cases, not that negligence is not a cause of action where the absolute duty is raised, but that the wrongful act of keeping the animal, with the other necessary elements, is a cause of action without the aid of the allegation of negligence.

The cases of negligence in the physical control of animals are illustrative of the general principles of liability in tort for negligence.

In Hammack v. White ([1862], 11 C.B. (N.S.) 588) action was brought under Lord Campbell's Act, 9 & 10 Vict. c. 93, by a widow to recover damages against the defendant for having by his negligence caused the death of her husband. The defendant had bought a horse at Tattersall's and the next day was trying it in Finsbury Circus when, from some unexplained cause, the horse became restive and, notwithstanding defendant's well-directed efforts to control it, ran upon the pavement and killed plaintiff's husband. The case was tried in the Lord Mayor's Court and resulted in a nonsuit, the Recorder being of opinion that there was nothing in the evidence to warrant a jury in finding that the defendant had been guilty of negligence.

The Court of Common Pleas subsequently refused to grant a new trial which was asked for on the ground of misdirection. Chief Justice Erle said: "I am of opinion that the plaintiff in a case of this sort is not entitled to have his case left to the jury unless he gives some affirmative evidence that there has been negligence on the part of the defendant. The sort of negligence imputed here, is either that the defendant was unskilful in the management of the horse or imprudent in taking a vicious animal, or one with whose propensities or temper he was not sufficiently acquainted, into a populous neighbourhood." After referring to the facts proved, his lordship continued: "I can see nothing in this evidence to show that the defendant was unskilful as a rider or in the management of a horse. There is nothing which satisfies my mind affirmatively that the defendant was not quite capable of riding so as to justify him in being with his horse at the place in question....It is said that the defendant was not justified in riding in that place a horse whose temper he was unacquainted with. But I am of opinion that a man is not to be charged with want of caution because he buys a horse without having had any previous experience of him." And per Williams J.: "It is said that prima facie the defendant was guilty of negligence because he was wrongfully on the foot-pavement. But the fact of his being on the foot-pavement is nothing unless he was there voluntarily; and, to say the least, it is quite as consistent with the facts proved that he was there involuntarily as that he was there by his own mismanagement....Where the evidence given is equally consistent with the existence or non-existence of negligence, it is **not** competent to the judge to leave the matter to **the** jury." If the horse had been entirely **unmanageable** to the knowledge of the defendant different considerations would have been applicable. The term 'scienter' would seem not to be properly used in such case, although Williams J. adopts it. (Cf. Manzoni v. Douglas [1880], L.R. 6 Q.B.D. 145.)

Attempts have at times been made to establish in similar cases, where the act is not wrongful, a liability in trespass, independently of negligence, upon the archaic principle that a person must answer for all the direct consequences of his voluntary acts. The early cases show a fair amount of authority for the existence of such a principle, though no decision goes to the length of actually adopting it. In every case the question will be found upon examination to resolve itself into one of pleading or the form of the action to be adopted. The decline of opinion towards the existence of the principle connotes the gradual recognition of the defence of inevitable accident[1]. At the risk of a digression it is proposed to examine those of the cases which relate to animals.

An early case, Gibbons v. Pepper ([1695], 2 Salk. 638) is in point. "In trespass and assault, etc., the defendant pleaded that he was riding a horse in the King's Highway, and that the horse being frightened ran away with him, and that the plaintiff and others were called to, to go out of the way, and did not; and the horse ran upon the plaintiff against his will, etc.

---

[1] See Pollock's *Law of Torts*, 6th edn. pp. 131 to 146, for a full discussion of the matter.

III] *other Animals, and Damage to Goods*   141

The plaintiff demurred, and had judgment; not but if the defendant had pleaded not guilty, this matter might have acquitted him upon evidence; but the reason of their judgment was, because the defendant justified a trespass, and does not confess it; for if A beats my horse, by which he runs on another, A is the trespasser, and the rider is not." The case clearly shows that the defendant was not even prima facie a trespasser. The matter of defence should have been raised on the general issue.

Wakeman v. Robinson ([1823], 1 Bing. 213) and Hall v. Fearnley ([1842], 3 Q.B. 919) raise the same point. In the former case the jury were directed that the action being one of trespass, if the injury were occasioned by an immediate act of the defendant, it was immaterial whether that act was wilful or accidental. They were not asked to consider whether the accident was occasioned by any negligence or default on the part of the defendant, or whether it was wholly unavoidable, nor was any request made by defendant's counsel that this should be put to the jury. A verdict having been found for the plaintiff, a rule nisi for a new trial was obtained on the ground of misdirection but was subsequently discharged upon reasons fully stated in the judgment of Dallas C.J. "If the accident happened entirely without default on the part of the defendant, or blame imputable to him, the action does not lie; but, under all the circumstances that belong to it, I regret that this case comes before the Court. The action was trespass, and the trespass was clearly made out against the defendant. It has been contended, indeed, that the defendant would not have been liable under any form of action; but upon the facts of the case, if I had presided at the trial, I should have directed the jury that the plaintiff was entitled to a verdict, because the accident was clearly occasioned by the default of the defendant. The weight of evidence was all that way."

An earlier case of Leame v. Bray ([1803], 3 East 593) cited in argument, was a case of collision between vehicles resulting in personal injury to the plaintiff. The report states that the accident happened owing to the defendant, on a dark night, driving his carriage on the wrong side of the road, and the parties not being able to see each other, "but it did not appear that blame was imputable to the defendant in any other respect as to the manner of his driving. It was, therefore, objected for the defendant that, the injury having happened from negligence and not wilfully, the proper remedy was by an action on the case and not of trespass vi et armis. The plaintiff was thereupon nonsuited." On the argument of the rule to set aside the nonsuit, the discussion turned solely upon the question whether the injury was "immediate from defendant's act, or consequential only from it," and the result was that the nonsuit was set aside. But the report clearly shows that there was evidence upon which a jury might have inferred negligence, and defendant's counsel assumed it in the objection which was subsequently upheld. But if the judgments delivered are looked at, nothing will be found there to show that in the absence of negligence the Court would have held the defendant liable either in trespass or in case.

The point arose directly in Holmes v. Mather ([1875], L.R. 10 Exch. 261), a case of a runaway horse and carriage causing injury to a foot passenger. It was there contended that the act of the defendant's groom in directing the horses on to the plaintiff in trying to avoid running into a shop was an immediate act of violence, that defendant was answerable in trespass and that whether the injury was wilful or not was immaterial. The Court of Exchequer held that the action did not lie. Mr Baron Bramwell took the ground that for the convenience of mankind in carrying on the affairs of life, persons in the position of the plaintiff must expect or put up with such mischief as reasonable care on the part of others cannot avoid. He also maintained that the immediate act of the defendant's servant was not to direct the horses on to the plaintiff but rather to guide them away from her in another direction. "As to the cases cited, most of them are really decisions on the form of action, whether case or trespass. The result of them is this, and it is intelligible enough. If the act that does an injury is an act of force vi et armis, trespass is the proper remedy (if there is any remedy) where the act is wrongful, either as being wilful or as being the result of negligence. Where the act is not wrongful for either of these reasons no action is maintainable; though trespass would be the proper form of action if it were wrongful."

In a later case, Stanley v. Powell ([1891] 1 Q.B. 86), nearly all the authorities were reviewed and the Court decided in effect that in the absence of negligence, alleged and proved, an action is not maintainable for harm caused by unavoidable accident from another's lawful act.

Apart from the question of trespass, which may now be taken to have been finally disposed of, the ordinary principles of liability for negligence apply to animal cases, and therefore the complainant must prove affirmatively such facts as will, in the opinion of the Court, be capable in law of supporting the inference that the defendant has failed in the performance of a legal duty. In other words, there must be evidence of negligence before the province of the jury is entered.

In Abbott v. Freeman ([1876], 34 L.T. (N.S.) 544) defendant was the proprietor of a yard used for the sale of horses. Whilst the plaintiff was walking behind a row of spectators who were watching a horse then on sale, a servant of defendant led the horse by a halter down a lane formed by the spectators on one side and a blank wall on the other. There was no barrier between the spectators and the horse. When the horse was about ten yards from plaintiff, another servant of the defendant struck it with a whip to make it trot, whereupon the horse swerved into the crowd and injured the plaintiff. There was no evidence as to the nature of the blow given, nor as to the disposition of the animal, nor as to the manner of leading it, nor as to any custom of erecting barriers in sale yards such as that of defendant. On these facts the plaintiff was nonsuited. In the Exchequer Division a rule for a new trial was made absolute by a majority of the Court upon the ground that the case ought to have been left to the jury. The dissenting judgment of Pollock B. is to the point. After mentioning various facts which would have tended to show negligence on the part of defendant's servants if such facts had been given in evidence, he says: "It was open to the plaintiff to give evidence of facts I have mentioned, or of excessive whipping or of negligent holding of the horse. None was given. If I had left this case to the jury I should in fact have left to them the result, and asked them to assume from its unusual nature that something unusual and improper caused it." The case came before the Court of Appeal who reversed the judgment of the Court below, being on the whole of opinion that there was no evidence upon which a jury might reasonably find negligence on the part of the defendant.

In Jones v. Owen ([1871], 24 L.T. (N.S.) 587) the plaintiff, whilst walking on the highway at about nine o'clock in the evening, was knocked down by two greyhounds which were coupled together. The plaintiff had no time to avoid the animals and, as it was nearly dark, did not see the coupling chain or rope until he fell over it. The defendant, who had been exercising the dogs which belonged to him, came up a few minutes later and ascertained that plaintiff's thigh was broken. Plaintiff did not in any way contribute to the accident. It was contended before the Court of Common Pleas that the award of the arbitrator (to whom all points in difference had been referred without pleadings) in favour of the plaintiff should be reversed on the ground that a scienter should have been proved. But the Court approved the finding of negligence on the part of the defendant although there was no evidence of scienter, Willes J. saying: "I agree that they (the greyhounds) are animals of an ordinarily quiet nature, and a person is not bound to exercise as much care with regard to them as he would be if he possessed others of a nature known to be vicious. . . . This, however, is not a case in which we have to deal with the acts of dogs by themselves. Here the cause of the accident was partly an act of their master as well as of these dogs. . . . We have to deal here with dogs plus coupling chains, and I am not prepared to say that this was a proceeding on the defendant's part, which was not in point of law negligence."

Although there be affirmative proof of negligence, the action may still fail on the ground that the harm was too remote—that it was not the natural and probable consequence of the defendant's wrongful act. Thus in Bradley v. Wallaces ([1913], 82 L.J. (K.B.) 1074) it was held that where a horse, not known to be vicious, is negligently left unattended in a yard it is not a natural consequence of that negligence that it should kick a workman who happened to be passing it. Lord Justice Swinfen Eady said: "In the present case the negligence found by the County Court Judge is leaving the horse unattended. But no connection is shown between this and the accident. It was not even sought to be established that, if the head of the chain horse had been held at the time in question, or if the horse had not been unattended he would not have lashed out with his heels just the same when Bradley brushed by his tail. It was not attempted to be shown that it was the negligence which occasioned the mischief. The guiding principle is that a person is liable only for the natural and probable consequences occasioned by or resulting from trespass, or negligence; an injury suffered must be brought within this degree to give rise to a cause of action." (At p. 1080.)

As in the ordinary law of negligence, so in these animal cases the ordinary defences to an action for negligence may be raised. Thus the plaintiff may prove that the defendant has committed a breach of a legal duty, but the defendant may reply that the negligence of the plaintiff himself was the proximate cause of the injury. The negligence of the plaintiff, however, must, as in the case of the defendant, be a breach of a duty known to the law. In Catchpole v. Munster (reported in the *Law Journal County Courts Reporter*, December 6th, 1913) action was brought by the plaintiff, a farmer, against the defendant, a taxi-cab proprietor, to recover damages for injury to three sheep which had been run over by defendant's taxi-cab at night. The plaintiff's drover had charge of a hundred sheep. He was walking in front of the drove and his dog was following behind. The taxi-cab was travelling in the same direction, at a rapid pace and on the wrong side of the road. The County Court Judge nonsuited the plaintiff on the ground that the accident was due to his negligence in not carrying a light. On appeal, the Divisional Court (Bray and Lush J.J.) ordered a new trial on the ground that the judge was wrong in law in holding that a person who was driving sheep on a highroad without a light was guilty of negligence.

It has already been mentioned that the straying of animals from a highway, where they are being lawfully driven, is an exceptional case, apparently falling within the rules of trespass but properly being dealt with under the heading of negligence.

The rule of law is that, provided the animals were

lawfully upon the highway, their owner is not liable
for their entry upon private property unless it happened
through his negligence or the negligence of those for
whom he is responsible.

In 2 Rolle's Abr. 565, pl. 7, referring to Y.B. 39
Edw. III, 3, it is said: "Si mon terre soit ouvert al
haut chemin et les avers dun estranger enter sur le
terre ceo nest justifiable." But against this we have
the dictum of Catesby J. in Y.B. 22 Edw. IV, fo. 24:
"If a man comes with a drove of cattle on the high road
past where trees or corn or other crops are growing,
then, should any of the beasts eat from these crops,
the man who was driving them would have a good
defence, provided the thing happened against his will.
For the law understands that a man cannot control his
cattle all the while. But if he permitted them, or if
he let them continue, then it would be otherwise[1]."
The truth is that if such entry is entirely against the
will of the person who has control over the animals, it
is no trespass, or at least what is known as an involuntary trespass. "A man is driving goods through a
town, and one of them goes into another man's house,
and he follows him, trespass doth not lie for this,
because it was involuntary, and a trespass ought to
be done voluntarily, and so it is injuria, and a hurt to
another, and so it is damnum." (Doderidge J. in Millen
v. Fawtry, ante, p. 51.) In Goodwyn v. Cheveley
([1859], 4 H. & N. 631) the plaintiff's cattle having,
while being driven along a road, strayed into defendant's
field through a gap in the fence, and the defendant
having distrained upon them damage feasant, the

---

[1] Quoted from Kenny's *Select Cases on the Law of Torts*, p. 600.

Court of Exchequer held that the defendant was not
justified, unless the plaintiff had had a reasonable
time, under all the circumstances of the case, to remove
his cattle.   Bramwell B. dissented from the judgment
of the majority, but only upon the question of reason-
ableness of time for the removal.   He remarked that
plaintiff "had a right to take his cattle along the
highway; and when cattle are driven along a highway
if there are no fences to the adjoining land it is certain
that the cattle will stray.   That is an unavoidable
injury which persons whose lands border on a highway
must sustain."

The reason put by the judges for the exception, if
it may be called an exception, is given by Blackburn J.
in delivering the judgment of the Exchequer Chamber
in the case of Fletcher v. Rylands: "Traffic on the
highways...cannot be conducted without exposing
those whose persons or property are near to it to some
inevitable risk; and, that being so, those who go on
the highway, or have their property adjacent to it, may
well be held to do so subject to their taking upon themselves the risk of injury from that inevitable danger....
In" such "case, therefore, they" cannot "recover without proof of want of care or skill....." (L.R. 1 Ex. at
p. 286.)

The authorities were considered in Tillett v. Ward
([1882], 10 Q.B.D. 17) and the same view of the law
adopted.   In that case defendant's ox while being
lawfully driven through a street in Stamford, escaped
without any negligence on the part of the defendant
or his drover and entered the open door of an iron-
monger's shop and there did damage to the extent of £1.

The judgment of the County Court Judge in favour of the plaintiff was reversed by the Divisional Court, and Lord Coleridge said: "It seems to me that an exception from the general rule of liability is clearly established where cattle, while being lawfully driven along a highway, trespass on premises immediately adjoining the highway." And per Mr Justice Stephen: "We have been invited to limit this exception to the case of highroads adjoining fields in the country; but I am very unwilling to multiply exceptions, and I can see no solid distinction between the casè of an animal straying into a field which is unfenced or into an open shop in a town."

It is noticeable that all the authorities agree in the point that the cattle should have been lawfully on the highway as a condition precedent to the immunity of their owner. Accordingly in Dovaston v. Payne ([1795], 2 H.Bl. 527) a plea of bar in avowry for taking cattle damage feasant that the cattle escaped from a public highway into the field through defect of fences, was held bad as the plea ought to show that the cattle were passing on the highway when they escaped. And Eyre C.J. said: "A party who would take advantage of fences being out of repair as an excuse for his cattle escaping from a way into the land of another, must show that he was lawfully using the easement when the cattle so escaped." The principle seems general with regard to the straying of cattle. The defendant seeking the protection of the Court on the ground of the default of the plaintiff, must not be in fault himself. Thus Heath J. in the same case says: "The law is that if cattle of one man escape into the land of another, it is no excuse that the fences were out of repair, if they were trespassers in the place from whence they came. If it be a close, the owner of the cattle must show an interest or a right to put them there. If it be a way, he must show that he was lawfully using the way, for the property is in the owner of the soil, subject to an easement for the benefit of the public." And in an anonymous case reported in 3 Wils. 126, Wilmot J. observed: "If a man turn his cattle into Black-acre where he has no right, and they escape and stray into my field for want of fences, he cannot excuse himself or justify for his cattle trespassing in my field."

Whether a person's domestic animals are lawfully on a highway is a question which is more difficult to answer now than it used to be. Recent cases have cast doubts upon the law of the early cases as will be seen from matters which will be considered later.

2. There is no duty at common law on the part of an occupier of land adjoining a highway to fence his land so as to prevent his animals from straying on the highway. Such an occupier is therefore not liable for negligence if an animal of his, not known to him to be dangerous, strays on the highway and there causes damage. But where such animals are allowed to stray on a highway in such numbers or in such a manner as to cause an obstruction and to make the highway unsafe and danger-ous to the persons using it, their owner may be held liable.

In considering the case of animals straying from private property upon a highway, the all-important question arises, Is there any general duty to fence lands adjoining a highway? To this there is a clear answer in the negative. Apart from the case of nuisance[1], there is no such duty. (Potter v. Parry [1859], 7 W.R. 182.) This being so, the omission to fence whereby domestic animals escape upon a highway and there cause damage cannot be considered negligence or a breach of duty. At any rate, arguing from general principles one would expect the result of the decisions to be as follows: If the harm suffered consist in damage to the soil or material of the highway, then the owner of the highway would have his remedy in trespass. If the harm suffered be injury to a person or damage to property lawfully upon the highway, the complainant would have his remedy in an action for negligence, provided (1) that a legal duty of the defendant towards the plaintiff and a breach of that duty be shown, and (2) that the injury or damage complained of be not too remote, i.e. that the breach of duty was the "proximate cause" of the harm occurring.

The familiar case of Cox v. Burbidge ([1863], 13 C.B. (N.S.) 430) is a good illustration of the principles before stated. This was an action for negligence, not for trespass. The defendant's horse, being on a highway, kicked the plaintiff, a child, who was playing there. No evidence was adduced to show how the horse came to be there, or what induced it to kick the child, or that

---

[1] E.g. where there is an excavation on the land which is sufficiently near the highway to be dangerous if left unfenced. (Barnes v. Ward [1850], 9 C.B. 392.)

it had a habit of kicking. The question of liability was argued in great detail before the Court of Common Pleas. A rule nisi to enter a nonsuit was there made absolute upon the ground that there was no evidence from which a jury would be justified in inferring that the defendant had been guilty of actionable negligence. The question of trespass was dealt with by Erle C.J. as follows: "As between the owner of the horse and the owner of the soil of the highway or of the herbage growing thereon, we may assume that the horse was trespassing: and if the horse had done any damage to the soil, the owner of the soil might have had a right of action against his owner. So, it may be assumed, that, if the place in question were a public highway, the owner of the horse might have been liable to be proceeded against under the Highway Act. But, in considering the claim of the plaintiff against the defendant for the injury sustained from the kick, the question whether the horse was a trespasser as against the owner of the soil, or whether his owner was amenable under the Highway Act, has nothing to do with the case of the plaintiff. I am also of opinion that so much of the argument which has been addressed to us on the part of the plaintiff as assumes the action to be founded upon the negligence of the owner of the horse in allowing it to be upon the road unattended, is not tenable. To entitle the plaintiff to maintain the action, it is necessary to show a breach of some legal duty due from the defendant to the plaintiff; and it is enough to say that there is no evidence to support the affirmative of the issue that there was negligence on the part of the defendant for which an action would lie by the plaintiff.

The simple fact found is, that the horse was on the highway. He may have been there without any negligence of the owner; he might have been put there by a stranger, or might have escaped from some inclosed place without the owner's knowledge. To entitle the plaintiff to recover there must be some affirmative proof of negligence in the defendant in respect of a duty owing to the plaintiff." And he went on to hold that even if there was any negligence on the part of the owner of the horse it was not connected in any way with the damage of which the plaintiff complained.

It is material to consider carefully the remarks of the learned judge or the true grounds of the decision may escape notice. The rule for a nonsuit was made absolute upon the ground (1) that there was no evidence to support an allegation of negligence—not, that even if negligence were shown no cause of action would arise; and (2) that supposing negligence were established, then it was not at all connected with the damage of which the plaintiff complained, i.e. that the damage was too remote. The mere fact of an animal being found unattended in the highway cannot be regarded as making the owner liable for the consequences. In an American case the conditions were thus laid down generally: "In order to constitute the being there of such animals wrongful on the part of the owner, it should appear that the circumstances and occasion or that the character and habits of the animal were such as to show carelessness on the part of such owner in reference to the convenience and safety of travellers on such highway." (Holden v. Shattuck, 34 Verm. 336.)

In English law if there is negligence then the sole question is, Was the harm too remote? With the scienter, as such, the law of negligence has nothing to do. Where the act of the animal which causes harm is not a vicious act but one within the ordinary nature of the animal to commit, the owner may still be liable, not indeed on the grounds laid down in May v. Burdett, but on the ground of negligence and proximity of damage.

Cox v. Burbidge was an action for negligence, and it is in this form that the remedy is sought in the majority of cases of animals straying upon a highway and doing damage there. But where the injury proceeds from a vicious act on the part of the animal whose character for harm is known, there is a breach of the absolute duty and the action might simply follow the lines of cases like May v. Burdett or Jackson v. Smithson, and allege the keeping of the animal, the scienter and the injury. Willes J. in his judgment in Cox v. Burbidge appears to adopt this position as the basis of the action and the ground upon which it was proper to decide it.

Here is reached the point where scienter and proximity of damage march together. With regard to injuries to human beings the matter is settled. Whether the action is for negligence or for a breach of the absolute duty, success will depend on whether there is proof of knowledge in the owner of the animal of a disposition to cause the kind of harm suffered. In the case of negligence, this proof is to establish proximity of damage; in the case of the absolute duty, this proof is to establish the scienter.

With regard to injuries to other animals or damage to property, the two matters show a considerable divergence. It is natural for one horse to kick another, at any rate, under some circumstances. (Lee v. Riley, ante, p. 38.) But no liability rests on the owner of the horse on this account, as the so-called rule in May v. Burdett deals only with acts which are not within the ordinary nature of a domestic animal to commit (see p. 71). But, introduce the element of negligence; suppose that in breach of a legal duty the owner allows his horse to be on the highway unattended, then if it kicks another animal or causes damage to property it is submitted that the owner is liable and that proof of scienter is unnecessary. The act being a natural one to the horse, the damage is not too remote (Lee v. Riley; Ellis v. Loftus Iron Co.), and all the elements of legal responsibility are present.

Some such principles as the above seem to underlie the more recent cases, which it is now proposed to examine.

In the case of Hadwell v. Righton ([1907], 76 L.J.(K.B.) 891) some fowls belonging to defendant, whose premises adjoined the highway, whilst straying on the highway were frightened by a dog belonging to another person. One of the fowls flew across the road and struck the spokes of a bicycle with the result that the cyclist was upset and the bicycle damaged. The County Court Judge gave judgment for defendant on the ground that an accident of such a nature was not a natural or likely consequence of allowing fowls to be on the road. A Divisional Court dismissed an appeal from the decision. Phillimore J. there adopted the view of

Erle C.J. in Cox v. Burbidge, that there was no
sufficient proof of negligence in the defendant in
respect of a duty owing to the plaintiff and that,
further, the negligence, if any, of allowing the fowl to
be on the highway was in no way connected with the
damage done: Causa proxima non remota spectatur.
Bray J. pointed out the true distinction between cases
of animals straying on private property, and cases of
animals straying on a highway: "I do not think we
could decide this case in the plaintiff's favour without
practically overruling Cox v. Burbidge. We have not
the power to do that; and if we had, I certainly should
not say that case was otherwise than perfectly good
law. It was sought to distinguish that case by saying
that the fowls in this case were trespassing on the
highway, and the cases of Lee v. Riley and Ellis v.
Loftus Iron Co. were cited. But an action for trespass
can only be brought by the owner of the soil upon which
the horses trespassed, and the decisions were based on
that ground. Therefore those cases do not apply in
the present case, because this cyclist had no interest
in the highway, and could not have sued the owner of
the fowl as a trespasser. The only ground upon which
this case can be put, if at all, is that of negligence, and
upon such grounds as were stated in the judgments in
Harris v. Mobbs ([1878], 3 Exch. Div. 273)...." In
that case a van had been left on the side of the road
and this frightened a horse and caused it to shy and
kick its driver to death. Judgment was given for
the plaintiff in an action for negligence, upon the
ground that there was an unreasonable and dangerous
occupation of a part of the highway amounting to an

obstruction and a prevention of its free user by the public to an extent which was unreasonable.

In applying the test of Harris v. Mobbs, Bray J. said: "It seems to me that the element of danger is absolutely necessary in order to prove the existence of negligence. It is negligent, if at all, because the practice might be dangerous to somebody passing along the highway. I altogether decline to hold as a matter of law, or without evidence, as a matter of fact, that the presence of fowls on the highway constitutes a danger."

It is noticeable that in the principal case nothing was said as to scienter. Probably it is within the ordinary nature of a fowl to get in the way of passengers upon the highway, but apparently the Court did not think so. The question was solved by the application of the test of remoteness of damage[1].

[1] The case is further of importance in that both judges gave utterance to opinions which seem to have taken lawyers somewhat by surprise, with regard to the improper user of a highway resulting in damage to particular individuals. It was generally understood to be the law that the lawful use of a highway was limited to a right of passing and repassing. Any other user amounted to an unreasonable user and might be the ground of an action of trespass by the owner of the soil of the highway. This followed from the judgments delivered in the often-cited case of Dovaston v. Payne ([1795] 2 H.Bl. 527). There Buller J. made the following cryptic remark: "Whether the plaintiff was a trespasser or not depends on the fact whether he was passing and repassing and using the road as a highway, or whether his cattle were in the road as trespassers." And again, Heath J. said: "If it be a way, he must show he was lawfully using the way; for the property is in the owner of the soil, subject to an easement for the benefit of the public."

The decision in the case of Dovaston v. Payne was cited with approval by the Court in the case of Harrison v. Duke of Rutland ([1893] 1 Q.B. 142).

In Hickman v. Maisey ([1900] 1 Q.B. 752) the Court allowed that the public enjoyment of highways is not limited to a mere right of

In the case of Higgins v. Searle, decided by the Court of Appeal (Cozens-Hardy M.R., Fletcher Moulton and Buckley L.JJ.) and reported in [1909], 25 T.L.R. 301, the view of the law taken by Bray J. in the last cited case was approved and adopted.

The defendant's sow, which had strayed on a highway, jumped up from the side of a hedge as a horse and van were about to pass a motor-car. The horse was frightened by the sow and shied in front of the car which then collided with the horse and van and afterwards ran into a stone wall and was damaged. In an action for damages by the owner of the motor-car against the defendant, the jury found that the defendant was not guilty of negligence in allowing the sow to be on the road and that the sow caused the horse

passing and repassing, but includes other ordinary and reasonable acts incidental to the passing and repassing. But no previous case seems to have gone the length of Hadwell v. Righton. There are dicta of the judges in that case which seem to point to the opinion that the fowls though straying on, or even flying across, the highway, were lawfully there. It is true that no actual pronouncement was made to that effect but that was evidently the opinion entertained. Thus Phillimore J. said: "I think further that counsel has placed too narrow a construction upon the uses that may be made of a highway. I doubt whether the view that a highway is simply to be used eundo, redeundo, and morando for a short time, exhausts the uses to which it may be put. And certainly, in my opinion, though I do not think it affects this case, if fowls are kept near a highway and there is a piece of ground to which they would naturally and properly go on the other side of the highway, and they crossed the highway to go there from one part of their owner's land to another, if the land were fenced so that it was necessary for the fowls to fly across, I am not prepared to say that it would be an unlawful user of the highway on the part of the owner of the fowls to allow them to cross the highway in the natural way and at the natural height, even although in flying across at that height they might strike a person riding a bicycle or a horse."

to shy, this being the probable result of the sow being
on the road; but the jury could not agree as to whether
the driver of the motor-car was guilty of contributory
negligence.   On these findings the judge declined to
enter judgment for either party and treated the trial
as abortive.   The defendant appealed, and contended
that on these findings he was entitled to have judgment
entered in his favour, and this was the opinion of the
Court of Appeal.   The ground of the decision was that
of Cox v. Burbidge.   "No doubt a person who allows
his cattle to stray is liable in damages for any consequences that may happen from such straying.   But
liable to whom?   To the owner of the soil for damage
done, not to a third party or for damages such as were
claimed in this case."   The question of the disposition
of the sow was not raised on the pleadings, and no
evidence seemed to have been given at the trial in
support of it.   Negligence was expressly negatived,
presumably in regard to the defendant allowing the
sow to be on the road.   Whether the element of
danger was considered does not appear from the
report of the case.

The question whether the omission to fence so as
to keep one's domestic animals off the highway can be
alleged as the ground of negligence in such an action,
was raised directly in the case of Jones v. Lee ([1912],
28 T.L.R. 92).   There a young horse, which defendant
had placed in a field, escaped on to a highway owing
to a defective hedge.   The horse ran across the road,
and coming into contact with a tandem bicycle, fell,
and then jumping up, lashed out and damaged the
bicycle and injured one of the plaintiffs.   The County

Court Judge found that there was no evidence that
the horse was vicious, or in the habit of trespassing or
attacking bicycles or anyone on the highroad. He
also found that the defendant was guilty of negligence
in turning the horse into a field of which the hedges
were defective, but that as the act of the horse was
not one which it was in the ordinary nature of a
horse to commit, the defendant was not liable. The
Divisional Court dismissed an appeal from the decision.
Hamilton J. rested his judgment on the ground that
the injury to the plaintiffs was not the natural consequence of the defendant's negligence. Bankes J. put
the matter on higher ground. "He said that in order
to succeed the plaintiffs had to establish that the
injury was the result of some breach of duty towards
them on the part of the owner of the animal. First of
all, what was the duty of the owner or occupier of land
adjoining the highway with regard to keeping animals
off the highway or fencing in land. By common law
there was no such duty at all, and they had not been
told whether any such duty had been created under
the Highway Acts. Suffice it to say that by common
law the owner or occupier of land had no duty to keep
his animals off the highway. The plaintiffs seemed
to him to fail in establishing the first point—namely,
that there was any duty between the owner of this
animal and themselves, and he thought that the County
Court Judge was wrong in law in holding that the
defendant was guilty of negligence because he turned
this horse into a field with defective hedges. Be that
as it might, the plaintiffs would have to show in
addition that the horse was one which, to its owner's

knowledge, was of a disposition likely to cause the
particular damages suffered by the plaintiffs. He
thought that the judge had found even that fact against
the plaintiffs. The law, he said, was undoubtedly
different with regard to a stray animal which is known
to its owner to be dangerous. Such an animal is kept
at its owner's risk, and if it escapes, he is liable for
damage caused by it without proof of any negligence."

This judgment seems to be the most correct statement of the law. It carefully brings out the difference
between the requirement of scienter and that of
proximate cause, a matter which seems to have been
previously confused. It also marks the point at which
the duty of using due care merges into the duty of
insurance in respect to a dangerous animal. But it
does not deal with the question when and in what
circumstances an escaped animal constitutes an element of danger to the passengers on the highway,
that is to say, when its presence there is dangerous
apart from any question of the disposition of the
animal itself. This point was incidentally referred to
in the case next in chronological order.

In Ellis v. Banyard ([1912] 106 L.T. 51) the
facts were as follows. The plaintiff was cycling at
about 10.30 p.m. along a highway adjoining a field
belonging to the defendant in which there was a large
number of his cows. Plaintiff saw some cows coming
out of a gate in the field on to the road, whereupon she
slowed down to jump off, but was knocked down and
injured by one of the cows. In respect of the injuries
so sustained, she sued the defendant. At the trial
no evidence was given to show by whom the gate in

the field had been opened. The County Court Judge
held that under the circumstances the fact that the
gate in the defendant's field was open and that his
cows strayed on to the road, and caused the accident
to the plaintiff, was evidence of negligence; that it
lay upon the defendant to displace such evidence by
showing that the gate had not been left open by reason
of any negligence on his or his servants' part; and that
as the defendant had not displaced the prima facie case
made by the plaintiff, the latter was entitled to recover.
On appeal to a Divisional Court, Horridge J. adopted
the view of the judge. Phillimore J. held that the onus
was upon the plaintiff to show that the gate was open
owing to the negligence of the defendant or that of
his servants. The Court having differed, the appeal
was dismissed, leave to appeal further being given.
The Court of Appeal (Vaughan Williams, Buckley and
Kennedy L.JJ.) allowed the appeal and ordered
judgment to be entered for the defendant. All three
judges adopted the ground of the decision of Bankes J.
in Jones v. Lee and held that there was no evidence
of negligence on the part of the defendant. But
Lord Justice Vaughan Williams said: "I should be
very sorry indeed to say anything in this case which
might encourage the notion that there is no duty on
the part of farmers or cattle dealers and others to take
care and prevent cattle which are under their charge
or control from going on to the highway in such a way
as to obstruct the user of it and make it unsafe and
dangerous to those using it....I think that if an owner
of cattle by his acts makes the highway dangerous,
then that case (Harris v. Mobbs) is an authority in

point here that he may be sued. At the same time, I
am far from saying that it is impossible that a man
should be sued for putting his cattle in such a place or
position that the natural result is that they go out of
that place or position and if in large numbers obstruct
the highway and cause damage to those who use it."

Similarly Lord Justice Kennedy said: "I should also
be slow to infer that because a harmless cow or sheep
is allowed to get into the highway without giving rise
to a cause of action that rule applies to crowds of
cattle whose mass might constitute an obstruction to
travellers along the highway. There may be a case
of duty arising in the case of a mass or number, even
of the most harmless animals which would not apply
where it was only the case of a single animal."

It is not clear what is the precise extent of these
reservations. Animals which stray on a highway, it
is submitted, inevitably cause a certain amount of
obstruction so long as they are under no one's control.
If this be so, at what point is the responsibility suggested
by the learned Lords Justices to begin? Under what
circumstances does an animal, or a number of animals,
unattended by a human being, cause an obstruction
to the highway so as to give ground for an action by
those who in using the highway are injured by the
obstruction? It must not be forgotten that the lawful
user of the highway by animals received a broader
interpretation in the recent case of Hadwell v. Righton
than formerly. Apparently the view of the judges now
is that no obstruction is caused by a single animal
wandering on the highway unattended, whatever kind
of animal it may be, so long as it is of an ordinarily

harmless disposition.   Until a case occurs to explain
the meaning of the obiter dicta in Ellis v. Banyard the
result of the recent cases seems to be as follows: (1) An
owner is not bound to prevent his cattle or other
domestic animals from straying on the highway, but
he is bound to use care and caution that they do not
stray in such numbers as to make the highway positively
unsafe and dangerous for those who use it.   (2) If he
omits to use such care and caution, and damage results,
his breach of such duty must be proved to be the
proximate cause of such damage.   (3) If the straying
animal causes injury by a positively vicious act, proof
of scienter is essential.

3.   (1) The person who keeps an animal
upon premises in his occupation is under a
duty to take reasonable care to prevent harm
which he knows or ought to know is likely to
occur from the animal to persons who enter
upon the premises at his invitation, express
or implied.

(2) With regard to persons entering upon
such premises by the mere permission of the
occupier, the duty of the latter is no more than
to give warning of the likelihood of harm
from the animal.

It is now necessary to consider the duties imposed
by law upon the occupiers of premises in regard to their
safe condition from the point of view of other persons
entering upon them.   It should be stated that it is not
intended to deal here with any source of danger other

than the presence of a dangerous animal on the premises.
There are, of course, many other causes which may
render buildings and premises unsafe and dangerous
to persons entering upon them.   But it is not intended
to touch upon cases involving these except in so far
as such cases may be useful to explain the general
principles applicable, and to supplement the cases on
these points relating exclusively to animals.   The
subject under consideration involves distinctions in
the extent of the duties and the classes of persons for
whose benefit such duties are imposed.

And first, with respect to persons who enter upon
his premises at the invitation, express or implied, of the
occupier thereof, the law requires that the premises
shall be in a reasonably safe condition, i.e. as safe as
reasonable care and skill can make them.   The leading
authority upon this general principle is Indermaur v.
Dames ([1866], L.R. 1 C.P. 274), which not only stated
the duty in clear terms, but defined the persons to
whom the duty is owed.   Willes J. in delivering the
judgment of the Court of Common Pleas said: "We
are to consider what is the law as to the duty of
the occupier of a building with reference to persons
resorting thereto in the course of business, upon his
invitation, express or implied.   The common case is
that of a customer in a shop.   But it is obvious that
this is only one of a class....If a customer were, after
buying goods, to go back to the shop in order to complain of the quality, or that the change was not right,
he would be just as much there upon business which
concerned the shopkeeper, and as much entitled to
protection during this accessory visit, though it might

not be for the shopkeeper's benefit, as during the
principal visit, which was. And if, instead of going
himself, the customer were to send his servant, the
servant would be entitled to the same consideration
as the master. The class to which the customer
belongs includes persons who go (not as mere volunteers
or licensees, or guests, or servants, or persons whose
employment is such that danger may be considered as
bargained for, but who go) upon business which concerns the occupier, and upon his invitation, express or
implied. With respect to such a visitor, at least, we
consider it settled law that he, using reasonable care on
his part for his own safety, is entitled to expect that
the occupier shall on his part use reasonable care to
prevent damage from unusual danger which he knows
or ought to know; and that, where there is evidence
of neglect, the question whether such reasonable care
has been taken (by notice, lighting, guarding or otherwise), and whether there was contributory negligence
in the sufferer, must be determined by a jury as matter
of fact." On appeal to the Exchequer Chamber this
judgment was affirmed. The case also shows that there
is no absolute duty to prevent danger, but only a duty
to make the place as little dangerous as such a place
could reasonably be. On the other hand, it appears
that the general duty goes beyond the exercise of mere
personal care and caution. "Personal diligence on the
part of the occupier and his servants is immaterial.
The structure has to be in a reasonably safe condition,
so far as the exercise of reasonable care and skill can
make it so." (Pollock, *Law of Torts*, 6th Edn., p. 490.
See also Marney v. Scott [1899] 1 Q.B. 986.)   The

duty thus partakes to some extent of an absolute
nature. The duty, however, does not extend to
sources of danger which cannot be discovered by the
exercise of ordinary care (Hyman v. Nye [1881],
6 Q.B.D. 685); that is to say, to harm which is too
remote to be reasonably anticipated (Sharp v. Powell
[1872], 7 L.R. C.P. 253), or to harm the effective cause
of which was the act of a stranger (McDowall v. Great
Western Railway Co. [1903], 2 K.B. 331).

Such being the nature of the general duty, its
application to the case of danger from the presence of
animals on the premises may now be considered.
Reasonable care and caution must be taken to prevent
harm occurring to "invitees" from the acts of animals
kept upon the premises by the occupier. But such
harm only is to be guarded against as the occupier
knows or ought to know is likely to occur. This limita-
tion is practically the same as the test of remoteness of
damage in regard to cases of ordinary negligence. The
occupier cannot be held responsible for dangers which
he could not reasonably anticipate.

In Clinton v. Lyons (ante, p. 75) the plaintiff and
her dog sustained injuries from the bite of a cat which
was rearing kittens and was kept at one of the defendants' teashops to which the plaintiff and her husband
had gone to obtain refreshment. In an action for
damages for the injuries sustained the jury found that
the plaintiff took her dog on the premises by permission
of the defendants or with their acquiescence; that the
cat to the knowledge of the defendants, had while
rearing kittens a disposition to attack a dog in her
neighbourhood, and a person holding a dog; that the

cat attacked the dog unprovoked; that the plaintiff's injuries were the result of the cat attacking the dog; and that the defendants did not in the circumstances take reasonable precautions for the safety of their customers. On these findings the judge gave judgment for the plaintiff. On appeal the Divisional Court entered judgment for the defendants on the grounds that there was no evidence to support the finding that a cat rearing kittens has a disposition to attack a person holding a dog or that the defendants in the case knew the danger. It was also held by Ridley J. that the risk of the injury sustained was too remote to have been reasonably anticipated; and by Bray J. that as the plaintiff was not invited to enter with her dog but that she came in by the permission or with the acquiescence only of the defendants, and that as there was no proof that the defendants knew of the dangerous character of the cat, they were not liable. After distinguishing the case of a person 'invited' and of a person 'permitted' to enter and after considering the poistion of the latter, Bray J. continued: "No doubt if there were an invitation the duty would be larger (i.e. than the duty in the case of a person permitted to enter). It would be a duty to take reasonable care to prevent a danger which he might reasonably have anticipated.... If the defendants knew or ought to have known that the cat had a disposition to attack a person *holding a dog*, they ought to have anticipated the danger and taken care to avoid it. If I thought that there was evidence of an invitation to the plaintiff to come in *with a dog* I might have to consider whether the case should go down for a new trial in order that

11—5

it might be put to the jury whether the defendants
could reasonably have anticipated the danger." ([1912],
81 L.J. (K.B.) at p. 930.)

The liability of the occupier under the general rule
is excluded by the contributory negligence of the
person injured. But a more doubtful question is
whether liability is excluded where the plaintiff knows
of the risk of harm before he enters the premises.
This resolves itself into the question whether the duty
of the occupier is to make the premises safe or merely
to give warning that they are unsafe. In this form the
question is answered without difficulty. Mere knowledge on the part of the sufferer is no defence. It must
also be shown that he, appreciating the risk of harm,
voluntarily undertook to run the risk of it. (Smith v.
Baker [1891] A.C. 325 ; Thomas v. Quartermaine
[1887], 18 Q.B.D. 685.) Whether he did so or not is
a question of fact for the jury to determine.

Turning to the case of 'permission' as distinguished
from 'invitation,' what is the duty of the occupier
towards a person who is permitted to enter premises
where the occupier keeps an animal which is likely to
cause harm? The answer is that he is bound merely
to warn such person of the danger. The occupier is
not under any obligation to render the premises
reasonably safe to persons entering by permission, or
with his 'leave and licence,' as it is called. He is not
bound even to ascertain whether the premises in fact
are safe. His responsibility is to give warning of
dangers known to him but unknown to others.

The position of licensees was considered in Gautret
v. Egerton ([1867], L.R. 2 C.P. 371), where Willes J.

laid down a general principle which has since caused
the case to be regarded as the leading authority.   "A
permission to use a way is of the character of a gift.
The principle of law as to gifts is, that the giver is not
responsible for damage resulting from the insecurity
of the thing, unless he knew its evil character at the
time and omitted to caution the donee.   There must be
something like fraud on the part of the giver, before
he can be made answerable....Otherwise a man who
allows strangers to roam over his property would be
answerable for any danger which they might encounter
whilst using the licence" (at p. 375).   See also Hounsell
v. Smythe ([1860], 7 C.B. (N.S.) 731).

During the user of the licence, however, the occupier
is liable where he causes a new source of danger and
omits to give any warning of it.   (Corby v. Hill [1858],
4 C.B. (N.S.) 556.)   He would also be liable for harm
caused to the licensee by any act or omission which
would be negligent on the part of one person to another
having an equal right to be on the premises, e.g. where
he negligently drives over a person who has permission
to use a private road.   (Cf. Cockburn C.J. in Gallagher
v. Humphrey [1862], 6 L.T. at p. 685.)

A licensee may be defined as a person who enters
on premises by the gratuitous permission of the occupier
on a matter in which the occupier has no interest.   In
Southcote v. Stanley ([1856], 1 H. & N. 274) a guest
was held to be a mere licensee and one to whom no
'invitation' had been given.

The principal case in which the rule was considered
with reference to dangers from animals is Lowery v.
Walker ([1911] A.C. 10), which went from the County

Court to the House of Lords. The decision in the end
turned upon the facts of the case, and it is questionable
whether the judgments delivered form any valuable
addition to the law. Further, the case was complicated by the form of and the subsequent additions
to the findings of the County Court Judge. Plaintiff
had got over a fence into defendant's grass field in order
to take a short cut to a gate on the opposite side and
whilst crossing this field he was attacked and injured
by defendant's horse. The judge found that the short
cut had been habitually used by members of the public,
though without leave from defendant; that plaintiff
was a trespasser; that defendant knew the horse was
dangerous and that the field was habitually used by
the public, and that defendant was guilty of negligence
in putting the horse into the field; and he gave judgment for the plaintiff. The judge subsequently made
the following addition to his notes: "On the question
of trespass I came to no definite conclusion. The
defendant only occupied for fifteen years. I had
evidence of the use of the path for thirty or forty years.
The defendant objected and put up a notice fifteen
years ago, but would not prosecute." For what offence
he could prosecute is not clear. It could not be for
trespass.

The Divisional Court held that plaintiff was a
trespasser and had brought the injury upon himself,
and that therefore the action did not lie. Darling J.
adopted the test given by Chief Justice Gibbs in
Deane v. Clayton ([1817], 7 Taunt. 533), which was
approved by the Court of Exchequer in Jordin v.
Crump ([1841], 8 M. & W. 782): "We must ask in each

case whether the man or animal which suffered had or had not a right to be where he was when he received the hurt. If he had not, then, unless indeed the element of intention to injure, as in Bird v. Holbrook ([1828], 4 Bing. 628), or of nuisance, as in Barnes v. Ward ([1850], 9 C.B. 392), is present, no action is maintainable."

The decision of the Divisional Court was affirmed by a majority of the Court of Appeal. There Vaughan Williams L.J. held that substantially plaintiff was a trespasser and could not recover for harm suffered from any source of danger there might be in the field when used in the way in which such a field was ordinarily used, e.g. a bad-tempered horse or bull, but not a tiger. Buckley L.J., in a dissenting judgment, came to the conclusion that plaintiff was in the field without leave. He was in the position of "persons who go there without any right, but who, to the knowledge of the owner, habitually go there," and he held that "a person who habitually allows his land to be used without objection by persons who in law no doubt are tres-passers owes them a duty not to place on the land which he so allows them to cross an animal which he knows to be vicious and dangerous, without warning them of the danger to which they are exposed." Though the wording of the judgment as reported is obscure, it seems that the learned Lord Justice in effect held the plaintiff to be in the position of a licensee through tacit permission.

Lord Justice Kennedy, while holding that the defendant had tacitly acquiesced in the plaintiff's crossing the field, distinguished the case from that of leave and licence (as exemplified in Gautret v. Egerton)

on the ground that there had been nothing in the
nature of encouragement, inducement or invitation.

The House of Lords reversed the decision of the
Court of Appeal and held upon the findings of the
County Court Judge that the plaintiff was in the field
by the permission of the defendant and that in those
circumstances "it cannot be lawful that the defendant
should with impunity allow a horse which he knew to
be a savage and dangerous beast to be loose in that
field without giving any warning whatever, either to
the plaintiff or to the public, of the dangerous character
of the animal."

**4. A person who lets out for hire an
animal which he knows or ought to know is
dangerous, is under a duty to warn, not only
the person who hires it, but also any person
who he knows or contemplates or ought to
contemplate will use it, and such duty is
independent of contract.**

Liability for harm resulting from the authorised
use of dangerous animals is a case rather difficult to
classify. It seems best to treat it in conjunction with
the liability of the occupier of premises which are
rendered dangerous by the presence of harmful animals,
for both cases involve the violation of a duty of using
a certain degree of care or diligence, and both should
therefore be dealt with in relation to negligence.

Where a dangerous thing is delivered by the
defendant to the plaintiff in pursuance of a contract,
the liability of the defendant for harm suffered by

the plaintiff depends upon the terms of the contract between the parties. With cases of this kind and their application to the case of dangerous animals, this work has no concern. The defendant, however, may well be liable for harm suffered by a person who has no contractual rights in regard to the matter. Thus he may be responsible to a person for whose use the animal is intended, or to a person who the defendant knows is likely or ought to know is likely to use it. In either case his duty is the same. (Gautret v. Egerton [1867], L.R. 2 C.P. at p. 375; Farrant v. Barnes [1862], 11 C.B. (N.S.) 553.)

The general principle was stated by Lord Justice Cotton in the case of Heaven v. Pender ([1883], 11 Q.B.D. at p. 517) as follows: "Anyone who...without due warning supplies to others for use an instrument or thing which to his knowledge, from its construction or otherwise, is in such a condition as to cause danger not necessarily incident to the use of such an instrument or thing, is liable for injury caused to others by reason of his negligent act."

He is not responsible to other persons generally, but to those who he knows or contemplates or ought to contemplate will use it. Moreover, it is not necessary that he should actually know of the danger if he had the means of knowledge and neglected to acquaint himself with it. These two points were well brought out in White v. Steadman ([1913] 82 L.J. (K.B.) 846). In this case plaintiff's husband hired a horse and landau from defendant to take a party for a drive. During the drive the horse shied at a traction engine, the landau was upset, and the plaintiff, who was one

of the party, received injury.   In an action for damages
the jury found that the defendant knew, or ought to
have known if he had used proper care, that the horse
was not safe at the time he let out the landau on hire.
The Court held defendant liable as he omitted to give
warning of the danger.   Lush J. said: "A horse of
known vicious propensity is, as Mr Justice Willes said
in Cox v. Burbidge, within the class of 'dangerous
animals,' and the duty of a person who lets it out is
the same as that which any person is under who allows
others to use or come in contact with an animal or
chattel that is dangerous in itself.   He is under a duty
to warn not only the person who hires it, but any
person who he knows or contemplates or ought to
contemplate will use it.   The duty is not dependent
on and is not created by the contract.   It exists
independently of contract.   That which creates it is
not the contract but the supplying of a dangerous
animal or chattel for the use of another person....But
it is said that the defendant, who through his own
carelessness, did not use the means of knowledge at
his disposal, is in a better position than he would have
been had he used them and made himself acquainted
with the true facts.   In my opinion this view is not
correct.   I think that a person who has the means of
knowledge and only does not know that the animal
or chattel which he supplies is dangerous, because he
does not take ordinary care to avail himself of his
opportunity of knowledge, is in precisely the same
position as the person who knows" (at pp. 849–850).

INDEX

For EU product safety concerns, contact us at Calle de José Abascal, 56–1°,
28003 Madrid, Spain or eugpsr@cambridge.org.

www.ingramcontent.com/pod-product-compliance
Ingram Content Group UK Ltd.
Pitfield, Milton Keynes, MK11 3LW, UK
UKHW020316140625
459647UK00018B/1897